GRITS 'N GREENS
AND DEEP SOUTH THINGS

ALABAMA - LOUISIANA - MISSISSIPPI

PEOPLE - PLACES - RECIPES
WHAT TO SEE AND DO ON SOUTHERN ROAD TRIPS

BY SYLVIA HIGGINBOTHAM

PARLANCE PUBLISHING
P.O. Box 841
Columbus, MS 39703
Telephone: 662.327.4064
www.abookery.com
email: mail@abookery.com

Printed in USA

ISBN 0-9721032-5-2

Library of Congress Control Number: 2005908731

Cover photography:

Edwina "Mother Goose" Williams and Thomas "Bo" Howard.
Hodges Gardens, Many, LA (top right.)
Stanton Hall, Natchez, MS (bottom left.)
Beach scene on Alabama Gulf Coast (bottom right.)

CONTENTS

UPDATED INTRODUCTION
- AFTER HURRICANE KATRINA -

"Touched by the Hand of God,
To be Restored by the Hand of Man."

Grits'n Greens and Deep South Things was written and ready to go to the printer the week that Hurricane Katrina hit the three states featured in the book. Out of deference to the people who lost so much and the utter devastation of this land we love, we decided to put the book away, update it accordingly in a few years, and then distribute it throughout the South.

It's now a few weeks since Katrina and we're so moved by the prevailing spirit of the people of the region – and those everywhere who've sent aid and support – we decided to print now rather than two years from now. We did not change the inside copy of the book, so what you see inside is the way things were and the way we believe they will be again. If we mention an antique shop in the French Quarter, it was that way before Hurricane Katrina. If we mention an attraction or historic property on the Gulf Coast, that's what was there pre-Katrina, and we hope post-Katrina.

We see tremendous progress being made, and we see kind and generous people meeting unprecedented challenges wrought by the most destructive hurricane ever. We've seen the grace and goodness of so many, and we've seen anger and rudeness perpetuated by a few, perhaps because they lacked the strength of character to deal with adversity of this magnitude.

Hurricane Katrina wreaked havoc on New Orleans and the Gulf Coast region after it came ashore on August 29, 2005, and for days afterward. Walls of water came crashing in, destroying most things in the way. The devastation was massive, covering about 90,000 square miles, and its strength was unbelievable. Never in recorded history has the region experienced a Category 4 hurricane that packed winds of up to 145 mph. Not much could have survived the wrath of Katrina, which was compounded when New Orleans' old levee system was too weak from wear to keep flood waters out of our beloved New Orleans. Many people did not have the means to leave in advance of the storm and afterward they couldn't navigate through the flooded streets rife with pollution.

Initially, when the rains and wind subsided and the water started raging in the the streets and homes, a state of shock prevailed. Help was slow to reach the hardest-hit areas the first couple of days. By the time rescue efforts began, thousands of people were homeless, hungry and almost helpless. Now, we believe that hope is supplanting horror and restoration is underway.

After all, these people and this land are not strangers to hardship and struggle. But they take it in stride; they do what has to be done because they are survivors and they have great affection for this place they call home.

Biloxi, Mississippi, has been around since 1699, and it has weathered many storms, war, and famine. It's a major vacation destination in the South, with 26 miles of sandy beaches and casinos. We know the people of the Coast, and we know that they have the faith, courage, and the will to survive. We believe that they will prevail and their towns will eventually be better than ever. In Mississippi, we saw neighbors helping neighbors, and we saw more courage and fortitude than we thought possible.

New Orleans is one of the world's favorite cities. It's a special place known for great food, good times, jazz and joie de vivre. It's a city unlike any other, and though it is more European in ambiance, it is solidly ensconced in the American South. It's our place of the heart.

To all the good and decent people in this Deep South region whose lives were changed because of Hurricane Katrina, we wish you all the very best. Your courage continues to inspire us.

–The Publishers
Columbus, Mississippi
October, 2005

INTRODUCTION

The Deep South was a magical place for the Scotch-Irish, English, German, and Nova Scotia natives who came to settle the region. The "Southern Frontier" was previously inhabited by American Indians who eventually forfeited their land to the newcomers. Little of their influence remains. The character of the Deep South was formed by those who came from across the waters to carve a place for themselves out of a vast and remote wilderness that they began to tame and love.

Their influences – and those of the Africans who did not come by choice – remain in the Deep South today. See it in the heritage festivals, hear it in music, and taste it in various regional cuisines in the Gulf Coast states of Alabama, Mississippi, and Louisiana.

From tragedies to triumphs, the Deep South is unique among the United States. It has overcome the hardships of war and famine, and it has survived and prospered. Though the Civil War was fought in Northern states as well as Southern, it was the South that experienced more torched towns and homes. It was the South whose proud but rag-tag Confederate Army lacked the munitions plants that operated in the industrial North. And it was the Southern soldiers who came home to starving families, ransacked and ruined houses, and no crops, if they came home at all. Those who did changed their expectations, and survival took precedence over pride. They moved on, grew stronger, built great cities, and today, the Civil War is seldom mentioned. But it shaped our history, and we hope that this important period in forging a new nation will not be omitted from history books. Lessons are learned from the past.

It is our aim with this book to show that the region plays off its past and its diversity, and uses a bit of friendly competition to best advantage. Rivalries – from SEC football games to which states boast the most amazing antebellum architecture – keeps things interesting and lively in this very special part of the American South.

Writing this book has been one big road trip for me, because it has given me a chance to spend time in some of my favorite places under the guise of research. I've been writing about the South for about 20 years and I still find it infinitely interesting and forever changing.

We thank those who bought and asked for more copies of the first in the "Grits" series, *Grits 'n Greens and Mississippi Things*. It is now sold out, but a revised and updated Mississippi section is included in this second in the series. We have plans for books on Georgia, South Carolina, North Carolina, and Tennessee to complete the Deep South states.

People often comment on the name, "Grits 'n Greens." We explained it in the Mississippi book, but those who missed it, here 'tis again. As the very young bride of a dashing sailor in the U.S. Navy, we lived in Brooklyn, New York, while his ship was in dry docks there. Being a country girl from the deep woods of South Mississippi, I longed for tall trees and greenery, so we spent a lot of time picnicking at Prospect Park. Once while there, I heard a distinct accent and knew it was from home. I followed the voice, found the woman, and learned that indeed, she was from the Magnolia State, too. We talked about home and admitted to being homesick. She said that she was so hungry for good old Southern food, like grits and greens, and her Big Mama's blackberry pie. The down-South sound of "grits and greens" stuck with me, and I thought at that time that someday I would write a book and use "grits and greens" in the title. That's the rest of the story.

Please know that fees are charged for many of the attractions and historic homes mentioned. If you need to know before you go, we have included state and local tourist contacts near the back of the book so that you will have access to current information.

Thank you for your interest in our Grits 'n Greens books about the South!

Sylvia Higginbotham
Columbus, Mississippi

ALABAMA

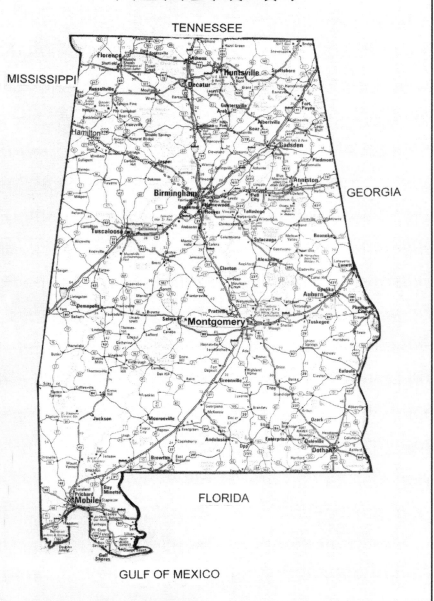

ALABAMA FACTS

- The Talladega Superspeedway is the world's fastest motor speedway.

- One of the best natural history museums in the Southeast is the Anniston Museum of Natural History.

- The Montgomery Museum of Fine Arts is renowned for its Blount Collection of American Art.

- Camden was the site of the Wilcox Female Institute, c. 1850, one of the first boarding schools for girls in the state.

- Harpersville hosts the great "Grape Stomp" each September.

- Alabama is a state that loves its food! Every month of the year, there are several food festivals going on. Some of the most unusual are Dumplin' Days Festival in Decatur, the annual Opp Jaycees Rattlesnake Rodeo (yes, they serve fried or grilled rattlesnake and say it's delicious), the annual Corks and Chefs in Birmingham, and many barbecue cook-offs, catfish festivals, and fruit-named festivals, as in strawberry and peach. Ask for a Calendar of Events.

- The Old Courthouse Museum in Monroeville has a courtroom used as a model for the classic film, *To Kill a Mockingbird,* written by Monroeville native Harper Lee.

- Gulf Shores and Orange Beach offer 32 miles of sugar-white sand beaches and emerald Gulf waters, as well as plentiful vacation cottages and condos.

- The Punta Clara Candy Kitchen in Point Clear has been making candy every day since 1952.

- The Oakleigh Historic Complex in Mobile houses elaborate gowns from past carnival queens in the Mardi Gras Cottage. These festive gowns must be seen to be believed!

- The Museum of Mobile is an excellent place from which to learn about the early days of the fascinating city of Mobile. Exhibits come alive in this National Historic Landmark.

- Perdido Vineyards near Atmore features wines made from native muscadine and scuppernong grapes. Find a hint of Italy with a Southern flavor.

- Antiques are plentiful in Brundidge, where seven shops are open, and Enterprise, with eight shops along the Enterprise Antique Trail. Additionally, the town of Foley boasts some of the best-known antique shops in the South.

ALABAMA

INTRODUCTION

Welcome to the Heart of Dixie! "Dixie" is not a word that we hear often because of its association with the Civil War and later the Civil Rights movement, neither of which currently enjoy the positive PC status they once did, but then, the term "political correctness" is passé, too. According to Webster's New Collegiate Dictionary (copyright 1951), the only dictionary in my possession that even mentioned the word Dixie, *dix* is French. The definition: *"A $10 note widely current in Louisiana before the Civil War, with a large F dix (ten) in the center of the reverse."* Perhaps 'Louisiana' refers to the Louisiana Territory, which was once controlled by France. Other definitions are, *"A collective designation of the Southern States of the United States,"* and *"A song composed in 1859 by D.D. Emmett, which became a popular Confederate war song and later a national favorite."* For most die-hard Southerners, however, the song "Dixie" will always be revered because it reminds us of a beautiful land, front porch rockers and genteel white-haired ladies. It pulls at our heartstrings as we fondly remember the place we call home.

Alabama is a state of beaches and mountains, hills and valleys, history and happenstance, and so many events that shaped the nation's consciousness, from the Civil War to civil rights. About 70 percent of Alabama's 45 million or so people live in the metropolitan areas of Anniston, Auburn-Opelika, Birmingham, Decatur, Dothan, Florence, Gadsden, Huntsville, Mobile, Montgomery, and Tuscaloosa. The rest enjoy the best of the rural South.

I am always amazed at Alabama's richness. Each of the regions are distinctly different in geography, lifestyle and cuisine. For a good look at the food aspects of this deep South state once known as the Heart of Dixie, pick up a copy of *Alabama Classics*, a new publication that showcases the unique foods, chefs and recipes of Alabama. To order, call the Birmingham News Company or the Alabama Bureau of Tourism and Travel; see listings at back of this book. The first lady of Alabama, Patsy Riley, introduces the publication. At the end of this chapter, we will feature a few of the recipes from *Alabama Classics* along with others we collected from our friends and their friends. Thanks to Ami Simpson with the Alabama Bureau of Tourism and Travel for introducing us to *Alabama Classics*.

Alabamians are generally friendly and helpful to strangers and they appear to be caring and compassionate to their own. Notice the colorful flowers that decorate cemeteries across the state. Someone in each community cares enough to keep the flowers looking fresh and pretty. It seems as though each grave is decorated with flowers and the result is a profusion of color that makes cemeteries look much less daunting.

Road-tripping through Alabama offers the best of all worlds. Big cities and all the amenities they offer, small towns and their peaceful front porches, beaches, mountains, music, rivers, lakes, fantastic festivals, and outstanding food at such special restaurants as the Bright Star in Bessemer, one of my favorites in the entire South. It has been in the same family long enough to have mastered the art of superb food and service in a pleasant atmosphere. And might I add, this is one of many fine restaurants to be found throughout Alabama. Seafood served in the coastal region is simply *c'est magnifique!*

STARS FELL ON ALABAMA!

How many times have you seen the Alabama car tags that read, "Stars Fell On Alabama" and wondered what it meant? Here's an account of the phenomenon that occurred on November 13, 1833...

Unbeknownst to those who saw it, the stars "falling on Alabama" were actually a meteor shower, sometimes called "shooting stars." After having been passed down from generation to generation, the story has grown in proportion. Apparently some thought the sky was falling and began to run to their horses for a great getaway while others fell to their knees in prayer! Either way, the people were terror-stricken.

Alabama Bureau of Tourism and Travel staffer Russell Nolen wrote this in a piece several years ago, "From the taverns to the plantations, pleas for mercy and forgiveness were being made as sinners became converted. That was the kind of night it was in Alabama, when the penetrating light of shooting stars illumined the darkened souls of men."

Again, unbeknownst to people at the time because there was no immediate response reportage, the meteor shower was observed in Europe and North America, though the climate conditions in Alabama were ideal, thus the stars that fell on Alabama appeared more pronounced.

Alabamians were pleased to see morning come and realize that the world had not come to an end! Still today, the night the stars fell is used as a reference for time, as in, "She's so old, she remembers the night the stars fell." Because of the curiosity associated with this fantastic event, it has been immortalized in books and song.

Since no one actually saw a star hit the earth, there was speculation as to what happened to them. More than one amateur astrologer said that perhaps they fell into the Gulf, and after living in salt water so long, they were transmogrified into the starfish that the Gulf tides push ashore today.

North Alabama

Huntsville

Huntsville is yesterday's old South and tomorrow's Space Age; it is small town charm coupled with a bold and vibrant tomorrow. It represents the past, present and future with aplomb and the spirit of adventure, which may have been one reason Virginian John Hunt settled here in 1805 and laid claim to the first English-speaking settlement in the state. Hunt must have loved the beautiful, mountain-backed valley, as did others who came later, among them Leroy Pope. It was here that the state legislature first met when Alabama became the 22nd state in the Union.

The state's largest antebellum district, Twickenham, is just east of Courthouse Square. Walk or drive the area and see the various architectural styles of the period, dating from 1814; some are open to the public. The Palladian-style Weeden House (1819) Museum in Twickenham is the birthplace of artist and poet Maria Howard Weeden (1846-1905.) The house features hand-carved mantels and other period design elements, as well as Weeden's watercolors.

See more of the past at Alabama Constitution Village, a living history museum that represents a working village of the early 1800s. Families enjoy watching the cabinet makers at work, the print shop, the confectionary shop and the library. This attraction takes us back in time, for it commemorates the place where the 1819 Constitutional Convention was held.

Following the traces of Father Time, head to the Burritt Mansion and re-live life in the Tennessee Valley from the 1850s. The living museum, Burritt on the Mountain, includes the mansion, a "dogtrot" cabin, blacksmith shop, church, adjoining farmland and nature trails, and an outstanding mountaintop experience.

See the way things were in 1879 at Harrison Brothers Hardware store, complete with a coal stove, authentic wooden floors, and hardware items that you thought you'd never see again. In business since 1879, it is Alabama's oldest hardware store and a real treat to visit

Huntsville was also the site of the birth of the nation's space program, begun in 1950, thanks to the arrival of German scientist Dr. Werhner von Braun and his team. They developed the Saturn V moon rocket and more advanced technology, which led to the formation of the NASA Space Flight Center in 1960. Today's U.S. Space and Rocket Center in Huntsville continues the space affinity so prevalent here. We've heard that Huntsville boasts more PhD's, per capita, than any other city in the United States.

U.S. Space and Rocket Center, Huntsville, Alabama.
Photo courtesy of Alabama Bureau of Tourism and Travel.

Join the world of the future at the U.S. Space and Rocket Center, where space exploration is what you'll find. The giant screen IMAX Theater is almost as good as being in space on a joyous re-entry to Earth. A hands-on exhibit lets you re-enter the Earth's atmosphere and land the shuttle! And that's one of many such forays into the world of outer space. This is truly a must-see adventure for families. Rocket City, USA, is the site of the Redstone Arsenal and the George C. Marshall Space Center.

There's so much to see and do in North Alabama! Just west of Huntsville, **Decatur** is a busy town on the mighty Tennessee River. It's also a great place to see outstanding Victorian homes, said to be the state's largest concentration of the grand old structures. See them in the Old Decatur and Albany Historic Districts.

Between Huntsville and Decatur, find the quaint old town of **Mooresville**. The oldest incorporated town in Alabama, founded in 1818, is today a postcard perfect village of that era. Actually, it is a vintage village. If I were a Hollywood site scout, I would stake my claim on Mooresville. It's too good to be believed, complete with small antebellum houses and wonderful old churches built in the 1820s and still in use today.

Good fishing is in the area — at various lakes on the Tennessee River and Guntersville Lake, south of Huntsville. Find abundant natural beauty plus boating and hiking. This is a popular site with outdoor enthusiasts.

Mooresville, Alabama, Methodist Church, built in 1817.

THE SHOALS

One of Alabama's most progressive areas is called simply "The Shoals." Here you'll find the towns of **Muscle Shoals, Sheffield, Florence** and **Tuscumbia**. Among its other attributes, the Shoals is well known in the recording industry. In 1965, singer Percy Sledge recorded the song, "When A Man Loves A Woman," and other recording artists followed suit. Since then, The Shoals soulful sounds have attracted such groups as Lionel Ritchie and the Commodores, the group Alabama, Emmylou Harris and others. See and hear more when you visit the Alabama Music Hall of Fame in Tuscumbia.

Ivy Green, the birthplace of Helen Keller, is also in The Shoals (Tuscumbia) and open for tours. *The Miracle Worker* is performed on Ivy Green's grounds each weekend in June and July. See the poignant play of how the infant Helen developed a high fever, then lost her sight and hearing. She was a wild child until Miss Annie Sullivan came to teach her to function without sight or sound. Their success story is recounted in *The Miracle Worker*. Helen went on to graduate from Radcliffe College. Here's a quote attributed to Helen Keller:

"When the door of happiness closes, another opens, but often we look so long at the closed door that we do not see the one that has been opened for us."

"Coldwater" is a name you'll hear around the largely restored town of Tuscumbia. The big Coldwater Books occupies a corner building, and then there's Coldwater Stagecoach Stop and Coldwater Falls. This is a good town for walking and finding treasures.

At Florence, the only Alabama house designed by stellar architect Frank Lloyd Wright, is now a museum. Commissioned by

Ivy Green, Helen Keller's birthplace, Tuscumbia.
Photo courtesy of Alabama Bureau of Tourism and Travel.

Stanley and Mildred Rosenbaum and completed in 1939, the house is constructed of cypress, glass, and brick and it's a Usonian-style prominent at the time it was built. I love the "no space wasted" built-ins in the **Rosenbaum House Museum,** which is on the National Register of Historic Places. It is open for tours Tuesday-Saturday.

This lovely state offers the best of the space age in the thriving city of Huntsville, and not too far southwest of the rocket capital of the world find the ancient and amazing **Dismals Canyon.** This National Natural Landmark is a treasure complete with pristine waterfalls, cool mountain streams, cabins, a country store that is nothing short of fabulous, and legends that will keep you on the edge of your chair. The name "Dismals" is somewhat of a misnomer, for the Dismals Canyon is far from dismal. The beautiful canyons are home to the rare little insects called "dismalites" that attach themselves to the damp walls of the canyon and literally "turn on" after the sun goes down. They create a glow over the canyon, and being there when the dismalites turn on is a most unusual experience. What a great trip for families!

The Dismals General Store, near Hackberry, Alabama.

Elsewhere in North Alabama, see quiet little towns, old covered bridges, a monastery, and a Benedictine Abbey at **Cullman**, the Ave Maria Grotto. The grotto represents a labor of love for Benedictine monk, Brother Joseph Zoettl. He painstakingly created 125 miniatures of world famous churches and cathedrals, all of which are located on landscaped hillsides at Alabama's only Benedictine monastery. The other monastery near Cullman is the Shrine of the Most Blessed Sacrament of Our Lady of the Angels. Read more about both later in this book. This monastery was built by Mother Angelica of the Eternal Word Television Network. More than 2000 visitors each week journey to the monastery.

Shrine of the Most Blessed Sacrament of Our Lady of the Angels Monastery, Cullman.
Photo courtesy of
Alabama Bureau of Tourism and Travel.

Ave Maria Grotto, Cullman.
Photo courtesy of Alabama Bureau of Tourism and Travel.

SHRINE OF THE MOST BLESSED SACRAMENT
OF OUR LORD OF THE ANGELS MONASTERY

There's a special place near Hanceville, Alabama, not far from Cullman, where the weary can rest, the discouraged are encouraged to seek hope, the down-trodden can ask for strength, the lonely feel the presence of love, and sinners find that mercy is within their reach. It is the Shrine of the Most Blessed Sacrament of Our Lord of the Angels Monastery — a place of peace and harmony, of goodwill and grace, a house where God lives.

All who enter the great doors of bronze framed by limestone arches and columns are amazed and curious. They want to know how it all began, why, when, and by whom? It's a long story, but one we'll try to capsulate here.

It began in 1995, when Mother M. Angelica was on a business trip to South America for the Eternal Word Television Network, hoping to find a connection in a place where many Catholics were losing their faith. Mother Angelica and the two nuns that traveled with her, sought the support of local priests and one in particular was most helpful. He escorted Mother and the nuns to the Sanctuary of the Divine Infant Jesus to attend Mass. After Mass, the Salesian priest in Bogotá, Columbia, took them into a small shrine where they saw the miraculous statue of Jesus as a child. As Mother stood beside the shrine in prayer, the statue appeared to come alive and turn toward her. The child Jesus is said to have spoken these words: *"Build Me a Temple and I will help those who help you."* Work on the Shrine began shortly thereafter.

Mother Angelica returned to Our Lady of the Angels Monastery in Irondale, Alabama, which she founded in 1962. She and the sisters started looking for a site, found the 400 acres of isolated farmland near Cullman, and went about building the Medieval-style structure reminiscent of Old World Europe. This site was chosen because Mother Angelica "felt the presence of God" here.

Construction began in July, 1996. Land purchase and construction was funded completely by donations. Five families combined resources and made an anonymous donation to fund the massive project, but they had two stipulations: they must remain anonymous and the amount of their donation must never be revealed.

The amazing artwork within the Shrine is international in scope and talent. The traditional work is intended to inspire devotion and reverence, just as the Romanesque-Gothic architecture was inspired by the great Franciscan churches and monasteries of the 13th century. The custom-designed appointments were crafted by expert artisans from various countries, among them the Talleres de Arte Granda in Madrid, Spain. The marble throughout the Shrine was fabricated by the Savema Company in Italy and Masonry Arts, Inc., of Bessemer, Alabama. Stain-glassed windows were made in Munich, Germany, and inlaid mosaics on the altars were created by artisans in Pietrasanta, Italy, who used a 400-year old method of hand chiseling and fitting. The statue of the Divine Child Jesus was sculpted of white Carrara marble

On December 19, 1999, the Temple was solemnly consecrated to God. In early 2000, construction began on the Castle San Miguel, which houses the Gift Shop of El Nino, the Great Hall, a conference center, a catered eating area, and several offices. The Castle complements the architecture of the thirteenth century Temple.

Mother Angelica, born in 1923 in Canton, Ohio, said that the Shrine is a Temple consecrated to Almighty God, open to people of all faiths. It is home to the Poor Clare Nuns of Perpetual Adoration, a cloistered Franciscan Order.

AVE MARIA GROTTO

The Ave Maria Grotto in Cullman County is located on the well-tended grounds of St. Bernard Abbey, the only Benedictine Abbey in Alabama and by far one of the most unique in the world. Unique meaning that this is where Brother Joseph Zoettel spent about 50 years creating the masterful works of art at the Ave Maria Grotto.

Born in Landshut, Bavaria, in 1878, Joseph Zoettel came to St. Bernard in 1892 as one of the first students of the newly founded college. He became a brother in the Benedictine Order and was later assigned to work in Virginia and Tuscumbia before returning to Cullman. While he was studying for the priesthood, the diminutive man of God was injured during construction on campus, and was left a "crippled hunchback" for life. The injury prevented his ordination, but he stayed to fill other positions at the Abbey. While working at the power plant, he began to collect odds and ends from the grounds, and used his findings to create little cement shrines.

After a while, the gift shop offered to try and sell Brother Joe's miniatures, and as it happened, they became popular items and much in demand. As their popularity grew, he needed more space to display his creations, so he moved them to the Ave Maria Grotto, which was dedicated in 1934. The Grotto is topped by an altar made of beads, broken jewelry, crushed glass, stone and cement. Many of the items he used were sent by people who heard of his work.

Brother Joe's work was even more unique because he used available materials to create architectural elements for his little churches and monuments. For example, he filled small glass apothecary tubes with cement; once the cement dried, he broke the glass and had miniature columns. He used such things as old toilet bowl floats to create domes and pieces of broken colored glass to fashion tiny stained glass windows.

He created primarily religious structures, one of which travelers to Rome will surely recognize. It is St. Peter's Basilica, and upon close scrutiny, note that he used an old bird cage to form the dome. See "Little Jerusalem" and other scenes from the Holy Land, St. Martins Church in his native land of Germany, among others. Brother Joe also paid tribute to his new home country by creating the Statue of Liberty and the Alamo. He eventually created 125 replicas, all completely life-like to the smallest detail.

The beloved monk passed away in 1961 and left the Grotto he so loved in the hands of others. He was laid to rest at the Abbey Cemetery. There is a small admission to the Grotto, open daily, and there is a gift shop.

North Alabama's mountain majesty is a favorite of visitors, especially in the fall when spectacular leaf colors range from fiery to fuchsia. This region is, after all, the foothills of the Appalachian Mountains. **Mentone**, in the upper northwest corner of the state up from Fort Payne, means "musical mountain." Indeed, these beautiful mountains do make the heart sing over scenery and attractions, among them antique shops, a dude ranch and ski lodge, a golf resort, and the oldest hotel in Alabama, the Mentone Springs Hotel.

Throughout the region, shoppers find great bargains at the Unclaimed Baggage Center in **Scottsboro**; expect to find luggage, cameras, clothing, jewelry, sporting goods and more. The outlet mall at Boaz — the *Southern Living* Readers Choice Award for Favorite

Shopping Place— offers 100-plus shops, and the Mountain Top Flea Market at **Attalla** demands a look-see. Here more than 1000 dealers set up on 96 acres and sell a variety of goods and sundries, plus there are about 2.6 miles of continuous shopping along US Highway 278. It's Alabama's top flea market and one of the nation's best; open Sunday only.

One of Alabama's covered bridges.

ALABAMA'S COVERED BRIDGES

The Bridges of Madison County have nothing over Alabama's covered bridges. You'll feel as though you've walked back to the early 19th century if you tour Blount County's remarkable, historic covered bridges. Blount County has earned the designation as "The Covered Bridge Capital of Alabama" because three of the state's twelve covered bridges are here.

Building bridges was a necessity back in the day, though covered bridges were not so much for looks as utility. Bridges were constructed with great craftsmanship and the best available materials as well as a covering for protection from the elements. Apparently the careful consideration and attention to detail worked, for most of the bridges have withstood the test of time.

The "pattern" for the bridges was based on the design of Ithiel Towne, a New Englander known for his unique "truss" construction prowess. The truss is built in lattice style, with planks forming webbed sides. The result is a durable bridge that can withstand heavy weight, luckily for us because the bridges were built for horse and buggy and small automobiles, yet they safely accommodate heavier vehicles of today.

The three remaining Blount County bridges are the Swann Covered Bridge, built in 1933, across the Locust Fork tributary of the Black Warrior River. It's a three-span bridge reaching about 324 feet across the rocky riverbed. Swann is the longest covered bridge still in existence in Alabama;

it is located one mile west of Cleveland off Hwy. 79.

There's nothing better than the sound of rain drops on a tin roof, and that's what you will find at the Old Easley Covered Bridge. The 95-feet, one-span bridge was built in 1930. This bridge is great for walking across and photographing. It's about one and a half miles from U.S. 231. Also in Blount County is Horton Mill Bridge, built in 1935 and one of the highest covered bridges in the county; it stands 70 feet above the Black Warrior River. See it just off Alabama Highway 75 in Blount County.

One of the state's largest covered bridges is near Cullman, at the Battle of Hog Mountain site. Built in 1904 and restored in 1975, this truss-built bridge has lattice-style planks. It is at home among shaded picnic grounds, a dog-trot log cabin, a grist mill and hiking trails. The Gilliland Reese Covered Bridge is near Gadsden in the scenic Noccalula Falls. It was constructed of rough-hewn lumber and covered with weathered shingles. Built in 1899, this bridge was carefully transported to Noccalula Falls in 1968. Admission is charged.

Covered bridges in the central and southern parts of the state are Alamuchee-Bellamy (1861), on the University of West Alabama campus at Livingston; the Coldwater Covered Bridge at Oxford Lake, near Anniston. This bridge was, according to legend, built in 1850 by a former slave.

Waldo Covered Bridge in Talladega County, east of Alabama Hwy. 77, was built in 1858, making it one of the state's oldest covered bridges. Its 115 feet spans Talladega Creek. Near Childersburg, find the Kymulga Grist Mill and Covered Bridge in the Grist Mill Park; the grist mill still operates along with a country store.

The Twin Pines Conference Center in Shelby County hosts the Bob Saunders Family Covered Bridge, which is listed in the World Guide to Covered Bridges. It is a 50-feet long and ten feet wide bridge of truss construction. Southeast of Opelika find the Salem-Shotwell Covered Bridge. Built around 1900, this bridge stretches 75-feet across the Wacoochee Creek. Otto Puls designed this truss bridge with latticework.

Before you make the Alabama Covered Bridge trek, check with local tourism contacts because accidents happen and the bridge may not be there. We went to see the covered bridge near Mentone and learned that it had fallen into the river. How sad to lose so important a piece of history, but in the process, we found the oldest hotel in Alabama, the Mentone Springs Hotel (c. 1884), with a big wrap-around porch, period furnishings and decoration. On site is one of the state's best restaurants, and immediately behind the hotel, a Victorian house sells fine and primitive antiques.

Mentone may be Alabama's best kept secret. Poet Sidney Lanier Gibson described it best in the poem below:

Mentone, a place the Great God built,
up near the sunlit sky.
There life is new and friends are true
and days too quickly fly.
Where wearied souls regain their power,
and sorrows leave with night.
Where peace is born with each new morn,
a haven of joy and delight.

CENTRAL ALABAMA

BIRMINGHAM

And then there's Birmingham, one of the Deep South's most exciting cities and one of Alabama's youngest. This busy city did not come into being until 1871, and since that time, it has re-invented itself from a steel town into a major medical, financial and business center in the South.

Back in the day (1870s), the busy industrial town earned the moniker of "Magic City" because it grew so quickly into a major metropolis. Today, however, the smoke stack image has been supplanted by banking and medicine. Medicine and medical research have helped put Birmingham on the map. The city boasts 21 hospitals; the largest single employer is the University of Alabama (UAB) Medical Center. As a leading medical and technological center, the city enjoys the financial contributions of UAB Medical Center, which is said to be in excess of multi-millions annually.

Expect to be busy in Birmingham, whether you're local or visitor. A favorite area is Five Points, where quaint shops, art galleries and trendy restaurants appeal to locals and their guests. This is the place to go for upscale amenities. Do check out the Birmingham Botanical Gardens, which includes the lovely Japanese garden. There's a beautiful profusion of color in this and other of the many gardens of Alabama!

The Alabama Theater for the Performing Arts is a grand and opulent place. It's a completely restored 1927 movie palace built by Paramount. Now, as a performing arts center, it houses the South's largest Wurlitzer theater pipe organ. For a great view of Birmingham, visit the observation deck and balcony of the gigantic Vulcan. It is the world's largest cast iron statue and it stands guard atop Red Mountain.

Arlington Antebellum Home and Gardens, c.1850, is literally a decorative arts museum with its 19th century furniture, textiles, sterling silver, and art. Once the home of Judge William S. Mudd, a founder of Birmingham, the house also features Civil War memorabilia. The architectural style is Greek Revival and the furnishings include a bed-

Vulcan Statue overlooking Birmingham.
Photo courtesy of
Alabama Bureau of Tourism and Travel.

room suite attributed to New Orleans cabinet maker Prudent Mallard.

Jazz is represented here, too, and so are jazz greats with ties to Alabama. The Alabama Jazz Hall of Fame features such musicians as Lionel Hampton, Sun Ra, Erskine Hawkins and others you'll recognize. The Birmingham Museum of Art is the largest museum in the Southeast. Come see why as you look at the permanent collection of more than 22,000 paintings, sculptures, drawings and textiles that depict art dating from ancient times to today. See the work of Europeans such as Rembrandt, Monet, and Gainsborough; Americans John Singer Sargent, Frank Lloyd Wright and others are exhibited, too. Of special note are the 18th century French decorative arts and the largest collection of Wedgwood china outside of England.

Racial strife occurred in Birmingham in the early 1960s, though the city proved its willingness to change in 1963 when civil rights and business leaders came to terms. Today, the Birmingham Civil Rights Institute houses permanent exhibits of the racial struggles and presents a good look at a past era. It contains excellent exhibits that make us realize how far we've come since the days of segregation.

See Birmingham's industrial past at the Sloss Furnaces National Historic Landmark. The 32-acre blast furnace plant once manufactured iron ore; today it houses a museum of the history of industry and a center for the creation of metal art. This city also boasts the fine Alabama Sports Hall of Fame, which includes personal memorabilia of most of the

Birmingham Civil Rights Institute.
Photo courtesy of
Alabama Bureau of Tourism & Travel.

200 or so sportsmen represented here, primarily Hall of Fame inductees with Alabama ties. This tribute to the state's sports legends includes Joe Louis, Bo Jackson, Pat Sullivan, Hank Aaron, Willie Mays, Jesse Owens, Pat Dye, Paul "Bear" Bryant, Bobby Allison, and many more.

The Southern Museum of Flight is home to the Alabama Aviation Hall of Fame and exhibits depicting famous pilots, among them Baron Von Richtofen, known as the Red Baron. See the early days of flight, Tuskegee Airmen, photos and aviation exhibits and outside displays of planes. Add to this mix formal gardens, nature centers, environmental centers, shopping, restaurants, and see why Birmingham is fast becoming a favorite destination in the South.

TUSCALOOSA

West of Birmingham, the University of Alabama at Tuscaloosa evokes pride in most Alabamians. Make no mistake —this is serious football country where the late "Bear" Bryant reigned as king for many years. UA is known as the "Crimson Tide," so during football season, "Roll Tide" is a rallying call. There are fine museums and plentiful attractions in this river city. Tuscaloosa served as the state capital from 1826-46. The University of Alabama was founded in 1831, and before the Civil War, fine buildings dotted the campus. Unfortunately, all but four were burned by invading Union soldiers. The Gorgas House (c.1829), is one of those surviving structures and is now open for tours

Women were not admitted to the University of Alabama until an educator, Julia Tutwiler, defied the men of the state and got women admitted as students in 1896. "Miss Julia" had political clout long before women were supposed to worry their pretty little heads about such topics as politics. Tutwiler, along with Bankhead, are recognizable old names in Alabama history. Hats off to the distaff side.

East of Birmingham, find the highest point in the state, the lovely Cheaha Mountain, standing at 2,407 feet. It's a favorite of hikers, bikers, and campers and the scenery is spectacular. **Anniston** is east, too, almost equidistant between Birmingham and Atlanta, and it is a town surrounded by rolling foothills. Downtown and elsewhere, there's a distinct Victorian flavor.

Between Birmingham and Anniston, just south of I-20, find **Talladega** and it's relationship to the NASCAR nation. Nearby is the Talladega Superspeedway, the world's fastest speedway and host of NASCAR and other high speed auto racing events. The International Motorsports Hall of Fame and Museum is here, too, on 35 acres of land next to the Speedway. Expect to see Indy-type race cars, Winston Cup Cut-away series cars, a research library, and gift shop. The exhibit area includes six halls of fame, including the Alabama Sports Writers Hall of Fame, the ARCA Hall of National Champions, the Western Auto Mechanics Hall of Fame, the Quarter Midgets of America Hall of Fame, and the World Karting Hall of Fame.

Talladega Superspeedway, Talladega. Photo courtesy of Alabama Bureau of Tourism and Travel.

In Anniston, once called "The Model City of the South" and named "Annie's Town" for the wife of an early industrialist, seek out the Anniston Museum of Natural History. It is one of the best in the South, with dinosaurs, fossils, and mammals in open dioramas, and even Egyptian mummies. Add the 400+ species bird collection, and plan to spend a lot of time here, especially if you have children. Most kids love the children's Discovery Room and the walk-through cave replica. The Berman Museum of World History has objects from Jefferson Davis to Hitler, as well as Asian art.

If you like a town that has a beautiful lake, a company that puts money into the public sector for the greater good, and pleasant surroundings, you may already know about **Alexander City**. The lake is Lake Martin, and the company is Russell Athletics. Lake Martin's 44,000 acres offer boating, swimming, fishing, camping, and golfing. No wonder it's a top choice for retirees. The Russell Retail Store sells quality sports apparel at discount prices; they're often called 'irregulars' but it's hard to tell what's regular and what's not.

In Alabama, you're never too far from grand old mansions, and two towns in south-central Alabama boast heritage homes and civil rights museums. **Demopolis** is the home of the opulent Gaineswood, a house museum that got its start in 1821 as a small cabin. Gaineswood went through a metamorphosis from 1843 to 1861 and ended up as a 6215 square foot centerpiece on a 1400-acre cotton plantation. The Greek Revival-style mansion fell into disrepair after the Civil War and for years afterward. Gaineswood is now owned by the Alabama Historical Commission and has been restored to the period of construction. It is a National Historic Landmark. Bluff Hall, overlooking the Tombigbee River, is also in Demopolis and it was built by slave labor around 1832. There's a restored log cabin on the grounds, and a gift shop.

Selma's history is linked to two periods of history containing the word "civil." The Civil War, because Selma was a major arsenal of the Confederacy — and Civil Rights, since Dr. Martin Luther King and his followers marched across the Edmund Pettus Bridge to reach Montgomery in the quest for civil rights. This important history is told at the National Voting Rights Museum and Institute. Today, Selma is proud of its Old Town Historic District, which includes more than 1250 structures dating from the 1820s and is the largest historic district in the state. Sturdivant Hall is here, too, and it dates back to 1853. It is now owned and operated by the Sturdivant Museum Association. Formal gardens and a gift shop are appreciated by the many people who tour the home year 'round.

MONTGOMERY

Next stop is the state capital of Montgomery, truly a city of diversity. From the first White House of the Confederacy to the Civil Rights Memorial; from the Alabama Shakespeare Festival to the Old

Alabama Town, Montgomery is a city that's ever-changing. Montgomery is also proud to be the home of Maxwell Air Force Base and the Air University. First stop here should be the Montgomery Area Visitors Center at Union Station, built in 1898 and now serves as an anchor for riverfront development.

The Alabama State Capitol is a good place to visit, for it represents the history and heritage of this great state. Learn more at the Alabama Department of Archives and History, and for children, there's "Grandma's Attic." In downtown Montgomery, Old Alabama Town is an authentically restored section of town in which each building serves as a living history museum

Old Alabama Town, Montgomery.
Photo courtsey of
Alabama Bureau of Tourism and Travel.

Alabama State Capitol, Montgomery.
Photo courtesy of Alabama Bureau of Tourism and Travel.

depicting the 19th and early 20th century. The Craft Center features working artisans, always an interesting look for children.

The prestigious Alabama Shakespeare Festival is an unexpected plus for this Southern capital city. Fans of Shakespeare flock here year 'round to see classical and contemporary performances at this state-of-the art venue; see more in the sidebar below. This city is also the home of the ultimate flapper, Zelda Fitzgerald, wife of the writer F. Scott. The unorthodox Zelda was a writer in her own right and according to rumor, some of F. Scott Fitzgerald's work was actually penned by Zelda. Hear more about Scott and Zelda at their museum, which is located in the house that served as their residence in 1931-32.

Enroute to the towns of Auburn and Opelika, east of Montgomery, pass through **Tuskegee**, the town made famous as the home of the Tuskegee Airmen of World War II fame. Today there's a National Historic Site in their honor. See also the home of Booker T. Washington, founder and president of Tuskegee Institute. Students and faculty built the home in 1899 using bricks made by students.

ALABAMA SHAKESPEARE FESTIVAL

You don't have to be a great fan of the prolific writer William Shakespeare to enjoy the Alabama Shakespeare Festival (ASF). It is not a once-a-year festival as the name might imply; it is, rather, a festival of year 'round plays. And it is indeed festive, for it celebrates a series of plays performed in a beautiful venue. The ASF building evokes pride in locals because it is an architectural showplace.

At ASF, the classics share billing with contemporary plays so that most theatrical preferences are covered. Recent offerings ran the gamut, with featured performances such as *Always Patsy Cline* to Shakespeare's *The Taming of the Shrew*; to Tennessee Williams' *Cat on a Hot Tin Roof* to Dickens' *A Christmas Carol*.

The New York Times called ASF ... "brash and brilliant." Indeed it is, and it's the only professional theater in the country that stages a rotating repertory of classical works with resident actors, most of whom are Actors' Equity members. Additionally, the ASF plays are staged by some of the top theatre professionals in the country, which is yet another reason the New Orleans *Stage Journal* said that the ASF presented "... excellent theatre in a spectacular setting."

The Alabama Shakespeare Festival is among the tenth largest Shakespeare festivals in the world and it attracts more than 200,000 patrons annually to the stellar line-up of classical and contemporary productions.

Actors at Alabama Shakespeare Festival, Montgomery.
Photo courtesy of Alabama Shakespeare Festival.

AUBURN

Auburn is the home of Auburn University, and this is indeed War Eagle country! There are several explanations as to why some fans call Auburn "War Eagles" and others say "Auburn Tigers." Actually, the team is the "Tigers" and the battle cry is "War Eagle," according to one reputable source. Whatever they call the team, we know that all fans eventually congregate at the historic and popular Toomer's Corner. Rumor has it that football great and former Auburn coach John Heisman often strolled to Toomer's Drug Store for a cold glass of their famous lemonade. The "Tiger Trail" is nearby. It's a series of embedded granite plaques that honor Auburn football players and coaches.

South of Auburn, the antebellum town of Eufaula is known for elegant old homes, among them Shorter Mansion, now a public home and a grand example of a neo-classical mansion. In the day, Eufaula's location on the bluff above the Chattahoochee River gave it importance as a cotton trade embarkation point. Expect great fishing at Lake Eufaula — the big bass capital of the world! Eufaula is near the Georgia state line and the Chattahoochee River. The Chattahoochee Trace is headquartered here; it's an 18-county river corridor that touts the perks of the region. The Trace office on North Eufaula Avenue is also a good place to stop for regional tourist information.

Auburn's Toomer's Corner.
Photo courtesy of
Alabama Bureau of
Tourism and Travel.

Alabama claims the moniker "Birth Place of the Confederacy" and "Birthplace of Civil Rights."

South Alabama

Dothan

If beaches and bays appeal to you, South Alabama is the place you'll want to be. Just before you reach the coastal region, the city of Dothan is a sprawling city well known to serious tennis players, among them USTA Pro Circuit champions. "Peanuts Around Town" are fiberglass peanuts decorated by local artists, each with a different theme. The art calls attention to the fact that Dothan is the peanut capital of the world.

Dothan's Golden Peanut.
Photo courtesy of
Ronald Searcy, DCMI.

Mobile

Welcome to Mobile, one of my favorite Deep South cities. Mobile has the pizazz and sophistication of a big metropolitan city and the charm and warmth of a small Southern town. Be prepared to be impressed, for the springtime flowers are so pretty they make your heart hurt. Mobile is indeed the city of azaleas.

This colorful city got its unofficial start in1519 when Spanish explorer Alonso Alvarez Pineda mapped Mobile and named it, "Bay of the Holy Spirit." Mobile, later named for the Maubilla Indians — was founded in 1702 by the Frenchman Pierre Lemoyne, Sieur d'Iberville. With the exception of St. Augustine, Florida, Mobile is the oldest Latin town east of Mexico.

Here's a little known fact: Mobile's Mardi Gras pre-dates the bigger carnival in New Orleans. When Mobile's Mardi Gras began in 1703, it was called Boeuf Gras (or Fated Ox). This time of feasting and revelry was the day before Ash Wednesday and the beginning of the Lenten season that leads to Easter. Mardi Gras was suspended during the Civil War, but re-established itself in 1869 with the Order of Myths parade. Today, Mobile's Mardi Gras is a big event, complete with Krewes, balls, and parades.

The flags of six nations have flown over the city on the bay since it was founded: the French Royal flag, the English flag, the Spanish flag, the Alabama flag, the Confederate flag, and the United States flag. Today, the flags form a combined shield on the city's historically significant buildings, thanks to preservation efforts began in the early 1960s. The historic districts include DeTonti Square, Church Street East, and the Oakleigh Garden District.

The historic districts — and all of Mobile — come to life in the springtime. Magnificent live oaks, shimmering with Spanish moss, create an enchanting back drop for the colorful azaleas so prominent in Mobile. During peak azalea weeks, usually mid-to-late March, the Azalea Trail Festival provides a 37-mile pink line that winds its way through the historic areas, giving visitors a good look at what makes Mobile such a special place.

Bragg-Mitchell Mansion, Mobile.
Photo courtesy of Alabama Bureau of Tourism and Travel.

Any time of the year, visitors can see the Museum of the City of Mobile, Forte Conde, the U.S.S. Alabama, the National African American Archives Museum, and a few of the architectural gems: Oakleigh, the Conde-Charlotte House, the Richards-DAR House, and the Bragg-Mitchell Mansion.

Patriotic Americans will find their way to Mobile's Battleship Park to pay homage to the "Lucky A" — the venerable U.S.S. Alabama, winner of nine battle stars for her participation in nine major engagements during WWII. Not only did the stalwart battleship engage — but she shot down many Kamikaze war planes near such places as Tarawa and Okinawa — without damage or personnel casualties from enemy attack.

When the proud ship was to be decommissioned, Alabamians, including school children, waged a campaign and raised funds to bring her home. Indeed they did; she now welcomes visitors at Battleship Park, along with a submarine, a B-52 bomber and a P-51 fighter plane.

Gulf Shores

In the Gulf Coast region, the beaches of Gulf Shores beckon those who enjoy the waters of the Gulf of Mexico, while others find their way to the Mobile Bay towns of **Daphne** and **Point Clear**. This writer spent many nights on a Daphne beach, waiting to see a jubilee. A "jubilee" occurs when shellfish, crabs and flounders leave the bay and come ashore. The timing is unpredictable, but it is said that jubilees occur in two places in the world: Mobile Bay and a remote part of China.

When you're in or around Daphne, seek out Malbis Greek Orthodox Church, an outstanding example of neo-Byzantine architecture, vibrant stained glass and murals depicting the life of Christ. A young man named Antonios Markopoulos, who studied for years in a monastery in Greece, wanted to share his teachings and assist his fellow man. When many from Greece came to America around the turn of the century, the young monk came, too, to help them apply the principles of the Gospel in their everyday lives. He arrived in Chicago and changed his name to Jason Malbis, and later decided to find land and make his dreams come true. He and a friend walked from Chicago to the South, searching for land to buy. They saw many

24

farms, but none were suitable, so they decided to stay in Mobile to work and replenish their funds. As they were contemplating their future while resting on a park bench in Bienville Square, the friends remembered the scriptural passage, "The earth is the Lord's, and the fullness therefore." It was then that they saw a sign from a window, "Low Cost Farm Land for Sale."

Jason had a vision that the land they saw, disappointing at first, was the place they were destined to buy, and so they did. The seller said that the young men could have the land, all 120 acres, for $10 per acre. They negotiated for a better deal and got the land for $600, with $100 down and installments of $25 per month. While clearing and cultivating the land, the two young men stayed with a neighbor and decided to purchase more land. With help from their friends, they purchased another 600 acres, and the Malbis Plantation business enterprise was begun. Greek immigrants had employment, their fortunes grew into more businesses, Jason Malbis continued his teachings from the Holy Bible, and the Greek community became more prosperous.

Their church was dedicated in 1965 to the memory of Jason Malbis. The interior features a 75-foot dark blue domed ceiling and remarkable mosaics; all artwork compliments of Greek artists. It is open weekdays for free tours, and well worth seeing.

FAIRHOPE

Fairhope makes one hope they can visit often in this fair city. Fairhope is known as an arts community, and it is the home of the Eastern Shore Art Center. Downtown, find more than 80 art galleries, boutiques, cafes and antique shops. The great Municipal Pier on Mobile Bay is a must-see, especially at sunrise or sunset. Nearby

View of Mobile Bay from the Grand Hotel, Fairhope.

Foley has museums, antique malls, and factory outlet stores. Point Clear has the Grand Hotel, known by Southern gentry as the place to be in the summer. It offers the Eastern Shore's most elegant dining. Whether you dock a yacht, play tennis, or just enjoy the scenery, the Grand Hotel is a Deep South tradition.

The towns so popular with condo owners and vacationers are **Gulf Shores** and **Orange Beach**, both offering white sand beaches, azure water, and a plethora of properties to rent along the 32 miles of seashore. This is a favorite spot for families from across the South. Thankfully, the area is coming back to life after a major hurricane.

Back across the Eastern Shore to **Theodore**, 20 miles south of Mobile, is the big and beautiful Bellingrath Gardens, where 65 acres of blooming paradise also offers a 15-room museum home.

Bellingrath Gardens near Mobile.
Photo courtesy of Alabama Bureau of Tourism and Travel.

The museum features Meissen figurines, Dresden china, porcelain sculptures by Marshall Boehm, and more. Sidewalks run throughout the park-like setting, once the home and gardens of the Walter Bellingrath family. This is one of the top five horticultural attractions in the United States, where six gardens are linked to bridges over flowing streams. Whatever the season, expect a profusion of color. A note to visitors: wear comfortable walking shoes.

Dauphin Island, three miles offshore, is a haven for anyone who wants to escape the real world. Once available only by boat or ferry, Hwy193 now runs to the island. The 15-mile long and two mile wide (at its widest point) island that sits peacefully between the waters of the Mississippi Sound and the Gulf of Mexico is a respite for anyone seeking R&R, good fishing and boating. Fort Gaines Historic Site is here, too.

Long before it became a haven for vacationers, the island was known as "Massacre Island" by the early Frenchmen who came into the area, for they found a mysterious pile of human bones. Today, however, the Audubon Bird Sanctuary, the only one in Alabama, covers 160 acres and is crowded with ornithologists during the peak viewing times of April and October.

From rippling streams in the north Alabama mountains, to the sandy beaches and bay of the South, Alabama appeals to nature lovers. Add the Robert Trent Jones Golf Trail — a series of outstanding public courses across the state — and the SEC sports events surrounding the University of Alabama and Auburn, and see that indeed, Alabama dotes on sports and family outings.

ALABAMA'S ROBERT TRENT JONES GOLF TRAIL

Though Alabama has long been known for excellent golf courses, the stellar reputation has been enhanced with the advent of the Robert Trent Jones Golf Trail. Serious golfers need no introduction to these marvelous courses, for more than likely, they play them. After all, the highly-touted series of public courses have golf legends associated with them. The legendary premier golf course architect Robert Trent Jones – with more than 500 courses world-wide to his credit – came out of semi-retirement to accept the challenge of designing the largest golf course project ever undertaken. Bobby Vaughan, former director of golf at North Carolina's Tanglewood, put together the "team" and began the process of crossing the "t's" and dotting the "i's" for making the RTG Golf Trail a reality.

Before that, however, there had to have been a sound idea behind this very ambitious project, and that came from Dr. David Bronner, CEO of the Retirement System of Alabama. He wanted to find a way to diversify the assets of the state's pension fund and make Alabama's coffers stronger so that the retirement fund would ultimately be stronger, too. He chose the multi-faceted economic aspects of tourism as the vehicle.

Previous interviews suggested that Dr. Bronner used the concept from the film *Field of Dreams*: Build it and they will come. He did, and they do. His plan works, for visitors will come if they're invited and if there's a pretty place, pleasant surroundings, fresh air and sunshine. In one word: golf. Better still, none of these world-class sites are more than three hours apart by car.

Thanks to Dr. Bronner's dream, since the first course opened in 1992, Alabama has become one of the nation's top golf destinations. Combine quality courses with value; add challenging courses for the best golfers and enjoyment for beginners, and success is sure to follow. Among the favorite courses are The Shoals near Florence, a hotel, conference center and spa where some of the 36 holes overlook the pretty Tennessee

River. Hoover's Ross Bridge Resort and Spa has an 18-hole course especially designed for tournament play. It's near Birmingham. On the Gulf Coast, Point Clear's Lakewood Golf Club is a 36-holel course affiliated with a favorite place in the South, the historic Grand Hotel.

The Robert Trent Jones Golf Trail begins its amazing trek to exceptional golf in the Appalachian foothills of Huntsville and winds its way down state to the Gulf of Mexico, all the while gathering player praise and media accolades. Various RTJ Trail sites host championship tournaments and the Trail has been named among the "Top 50 Golf Destinations" in the world by *Golf Magazine*; Alabama was named one of the top ten destinations in the world for golf by the International Association of Golf Tournament Operators, and *Golf Digest* ranked Gadsden's 18-hole Twin Bridges Golf Club among the nation's Top Ten "Best New Public Courses" for 2005.

Now the state has taken this golf success story one step further – there are now five hotel and resort locations, and some with conference centers. The two newest are The Shoals Hotel, Conference Center and Spa in Florence and the Ross Bridge Resort and Spa in Birmingham

The Boston Globe said, "In Alabama, a genius in course design created 18 jewels for everyone to enjoy at one-third the rate of comparable facilities." Green fees range from a low of $37 in December to a high of $67 in May, and remember, these are exceptional courses. *The New York Times* said that some of the best public golf on earth is here. That sentiment was echoed by *Senior Golf Magazine* when they said, "Alabama's galaxy of great courses will change your image of public golf forever." Indeed.

For information, see the web page *visit rtjgolf* or call 800.949.4444.

Robert Trent Jones Golf Trail's Oxmoor Valley, Birmingham.
Photo courtesy of Alabama Bureau of Tourism and Travel.

ALABAMA RECIPES!

Have you been to a family gathering or outing with friends where food was not the mainstay? The food served at Alabama outings warrant celebration! Read on, and find recipes sure to become favorites of family and friends.

The following recipes were collected from all regions of the state. Using seasonal ingredients, some recipes are real Old South, as you can tell by the way they're prepared. We drew the line when a recipe called for "lard" or required frying in oil, with the exception of Fried Chicken and Fried Green Tomatoes. Heart health is important to us and we kept that in mind when selecting recipes, but what Deep South meal is complete without something fried occasionally? The recipes follow the course of the meal, beginning with appetizers and ending with desserts.

ARTICHOKE BALLS

3 cloves garlic, mashed
6 tabsp. olive oil
1 (14 oz.) can artichoke
  hearts, drained and mashed
2 eggs, well beaten

1 cup Parmesan cheese
  (or Romano)
1-1/2 cup bread crumbs,
  seasoned
Salt and pepper to taste

Saute' garlic in olive oil. Add artichoke and simmer about two minutes. Fold in eggs and simmer again for two minutes. Remove mixture from heat, add cheese, mix well, cool. When mixture is cool, form it into bite-size balls. Roll balls in bread crumbs; bake at 350° F for about ten minutes. Should make 24 balls.

DILLY BRUSSELS

1 (10 oz.) carton small
  Brussels sprouts, frozen
1/2 cup Italian dressing

1/2 teasp. dill weed
1 tabsp. green onion, sliced

Cook Brussels according to package directions. Drain; mix Italian dressing, dill and onions. Pour mixture over sprouts. Chill several hours or overnight. Serve with toothpicks.

TIPSY WEINERS

1-1/2 lbs. beef weiners	1 cup bourbon
1-1/2 lbs. smoked sausage	1 cup chili sauce
1 cup brown sugar	

Slice wieners and sausage into one-inch pieces. Place slices in a two quart casserole; add remaining ingredients. Bake, uncovered, at 350 degrees F for three hours, stirring after first and second hour. Serve with toothpicks. Serves about 15.

CRAB MEAT CANAPE

One (7 oz.) can crab meat	Mayonnaise
1/4 cup finely minced celery	Toast rounds
2 tabsp. minced pimento	

Flake the crab meat and mix well with celery and pimento. Moisten with sufficient mayonnaise to hold mixture together. Spread on toast rounds.

DEVILED PECANS

2 ounces butter	1 cup pecan halves
2 tabsp. soy sauce	1 teasp. salt
Dash of Tabasco	

Melt butter in skillet over low heat. Stir in sauce and Tabasco. Add pecan halves to butter mixture. Blend well. Add salt. Place pan in 400°F oven for 20 minutes. Drain pecans and serve hot.

SHRIMP DIP

1 cup sour cream	1/4 teasp. paprika
1 tabsp. prepared horseradish	Dash of Tabasco
1/2 teasp. salt	Shrimp (boiled, peeled, chilled)

Add seasonings and sour cream; mix thoroughly. Place in small bowl on platter, surrounded by fresh, large shrimp.

FYI...Alabama's outstanding "heritage restaurants" still serve the best food around! Some of our favorites include Mary's Place, in Coden since 1926, where fresh seafood from the nearby Gulf is a favorite! And then there's the Dew Drop Inn in Mobile (since 1924);G's Country Kitchen in Huntsville serves up suberb soul food; Dreamland in Tuscaloosa makes barbecued ribs an art form; the Irondale Cafe in Irondale is THE place for fried green tomatoes; the Twix n' Tween in Centreville offers mile-high pie. Don't miss The Bright Star in Bessemer, it's been there since 1907. These are a few of so many!

ROLL TIDE SPINACH DIP

1 pkg. frozen, chopped
  spinach
1/4 cup green onion tops,
1 teasp. red pepper

1 teasp. salt
2 cups mayonnaise

Cook spinach, do not salt. Drain well; cup up with kitchen scissors. Combine all other ingredients and mix well. Serve hot, with party crackers. Serves 6 – 8.

CHEESE BITES

3/4 cup flour
1/2 stick butter (room temp.)

1 (16 oz.) jar Old English
  cheese spread

Combine butter with cheese spread. Work in 3/4 cup sifted flour. Form mixture into balls and refrigerate for several hours. Before serving, place in a 450° oven for ten minutes. Makes about 30 balls.

GUACAMOLE SALAD

4 tomatoes, diced
2 avocadoes, diced
2 hard-boiled eggs, chopped
8 stuffed olives, sliced

1 onion, grated
1/4 cup French dressing
1/2 teasp. chili powder

Combine ingredients with enough dressing to moisten. Season to taste with salt and chili powder. Serve on lettuce with additional dressing, if desired. Serves 6.

Alabama's Chilton County Peaches.

BING CHERRY SALAD

1 can sweetened, pitted
Bing cherries
1 can crushed pineapple,
drained (need two cups liquid;
add water to make two cups)

1 pkg. cherry gelatin
1 small pkg. cream cheese
1 cup chopped pecans

Heat one cup of the juice; dissolve cherry gelatin in hot juice. Pour a little of this mixture over cream cheese to soften; blend until very smooth. Add remaining cup juice and continue creaming and beating. Add remaining hot mixture and chill until nearly set, then fold in cherries, pineapple and pecans. Pour into mold lightly rubbed with salad oil. Chill. Serves 8.

ALL SOUTHERN GIRLS SERVE DEVILED EGGS

8 large eggs
1 teasp. vinegar
1/3 cup mayonnaise
2 tabsp. sweet pickle relish

Salt
Pepper
Paprika

Boil eggs in salt water to cover. Cook five minutes, peel. Cut into halves, placing eggs in a bowl. Mash well and add vinegar, mayonnaise, salt, pepper to taste. Stir in relish. Fill halves with mixture; place on egg plate, sprinkle with paprika. Chill.

TOMATO ASPIC

2 envelopes unflavored
gelatin
2 tabsp. water
3 cups tomato juice
1/4 cup lemon juice

2 teasp. Worcestershire sauce
1/3 cup finely chopped celery
1/3 cup finely chopped olives
1/4 teasp. Louisiana hot sauce
1 teasp. grated onion

Soften gelatin in water. Heat tomato juice and add gelatin, stirring until dissolved. Add all other ingredients. Pour into oiled mold or individual molds. Chill until firm. Serves 8.

DRESSING FOR TOMATO ASPIC

1 (8 oz.) package cream
  cheese
1 tabsp. grated onion

1 ounce Blue cheese
1/2 cup dairy sour cream

Soften cream cheese and add other ingredients; blend well with mixer. Refrigerate for firmness.

SOUR CREAM POTATO SALAD
From *Alabama Classics*

4 boiled Alabama Irish
  potatoes, diced
1/4 cup diced green onions
3 tabsp. diced radishes
2 hard-boiled eggs, diced
1/4 cup mayonnaise

1/4 cup sour cream
1 tabsp. vinegar
1 teasp. salt
1 teasp. sugar

Combine potatoes, onions, radishes and eggs. In a separate bowl, mix mayonnaise, sour cream, vinegar, salt and sugar. Mix lightly with potato mixture. Place in a covered bowl in refrigerator to chill at least one half-hour before serving.

BRUSSELS SPROUTS IN WINE BUTTER

1 cup chicken broth
2 (10 oz.) pkgs. frozen
  brussels sprouts
1/3 cup dry white wine

1-1/2 tabsp. butter
1/8 teasp. white pepper

Bring chicken broth to a boil in saucepan. Reduce heat, add brussels sprouts; simmer 10 minutes. Stir in wine, butter and pepper; simmer 5 minutes. Drain well. Serves 6.

BOURBON SWEET POTATOES

2 (29 oz.) cans sweet potatoes, drained and mashed
3/4 cup firmly packed brown
  sugar
1/2 cup butter or margarine, melted

1/4 to 1/3 cup bourbon
1/2 teasp. vanilla extract
2 cups miniature marshmallows

Combine first five ingredients, mixing well. Spoon mixture into a lightly greased 1-1/2 quart casserole. Cover and refrigerate eight hours or overnight. Before serving, remove from refrigerator; let stand 30 minutes. Bake, uncovered, at 350°F. Remove from oven, top with marshmallows. Bake seven more minutes, or until marsh-mallows are golden. Serves 6 to 8.

TOMATO BISCUITS

An old Deep South summer favorite if you have access to garden-grown tomatoes!

Biscuits	Pepper
Homemade mayonnaise*	Sweet Basil
Salt	Vine-ripened tomatoes

Make thin biscuits, bake and cool biscuits. Slice in half and spread mayonnaise over each half. Sprinkle with salt, pepper and basil. Peel tomatoes and slice 1/4 inch thick. Just before serving, place tomato slices between biscuit halves.

MUSHROOMS FLORENTINE

1 lb. large fresh mushrooms	1/4 cup chopped onion
2 (10 oz.) packages frozen	1/4 cup melted butter
spinach	1 cup sharp Cheddar cheese,
1 teasp. salt	freshly grated
1/2 teasp. garlic salt	

Wash and dry mushrooms, cut off stems. Sauté stems and caps in small amount of butter until brown. Line shallow casserole with spinach, cooked, drained, and well seasoned with salt, onion, and butter. Sprinkle with 1/2 cup shredded cheese; arrange mush-room caps and stems over this mixture, with caps top side up. Season with garlic salt. Cover with remaining cheese and bake 20 minutes at 350° F. or until cheese is melted and slightly browned. Serves 6.

Gulf Coast seafood extravaganza.
Photo courtesy of Alabama Bureau of Tourism and Travel.

BAKED ONION CASSEROLE

12 onions, thinly sliced
1 (3-3/4 oz.) bag potato
  chips,crushed
1/2 lb. Cheddar cheese,
  shredded

2 cups cream of mushroom soup
1/2 cup milk
1/8 teasp. red pepper

Preheat oven to 350° F. Butter casserole dish; place alternate layers of thinly sliced onions, potato chips and shredded cheese. Mix soup, milk and red pepper; pour over onions. Bake one hour. *Great with roast beef!* Serves 10 to 12.

POTATOES ROMANOFF

6 large potatoes
1 pint dairy sour cream
1 bunch green onions,
  chopped
1-1/2 cups shredded Cheddar cheese

1 teasp. salt
1/4 teasp. pepper
Paprika

Boil potatoes in jackets; cool completely. Peel and shred potatoes; mix with other ingredients except paprika. Bake at 375° F. for 30 minutes. Serves 12. *May be prepared the day before.*

PICKLED OKRA

2 lbs. tender Alabama okra
5 pods hot red or green
  pepper
5 cloves garlic, peeled

3 cups white vinegar
6 tabsp. pure granulated salt
1 tabsp. celery or mustard seed

Wash okra and pack in five hot, sterilized jars. Put one pepper pod and one clove garlic in each jar. Bring remaining ingredients and one cup water to a boil. Pour over okra, to within one inch of top of jar and seal. Process for five minutes in boiling water bath (do not use pressure cooker.) An *Alabama Classics* recipe.

FYI... Like *Southern fried pies? Southern Fried Pies in Cullman, makes made-from-scratch fried pies with fruit grown in a family orchard. The company also makes apple cider, apple jelly and an assortment of jams. Thanks to the Steele family for keeping an Alabama tradition alive.*

SQUASH DRESSING

3 cups cooked yellow squash
3 cups cooked, crumbled
  cornbread
1/4 cup butter or margarine

1 can cream of chicken soup
1 egg, beaten
1 (2-1/4 oz.) pkg. sliced almonds

Combine squash and cornbread; chop onion and sauté in margarine until tender; add to squash mixture; stir in soup, egg, salt, and pepper; top with almonds if desired. Bake at 400° F. for 40 minutes. Serves 6 to 8. *May be prepared day before and refrigerated.*

FRIED GREEN TOMATOES

4 or 5 green tomato
Flour and corn meal

Pepper
Vegetable oil
Salt

Wash tomatoes and cut in 1/4 to 1/2 inch slices. Wet slices so that batter will stick. Heat oil in small deep fryer. Roll in mixture of salt, pepper, flour and meal (twice as much corn meal as flour) and fry slowly in oil until golden brown. Serves 4 to 6.

TOMATOES

Alabama's signature side dish is without a doubt the home-grown tomato. Whether picked fully ripened to a rich crimson — no, the University of Alabama "Crimson Tide" did not derive its name from the tomato — or prematurely green, Alabamians love their tomatoes. Whether planted as a primary crop, in small plots in a backyard, or as a patio potted plant, they are prominent throughout the state.

Not only do Alabamians cherish tomatoes as a food staple, they also use them as gifts. As soon as they have one more than they can eat, they leave them on neighbors' porches or other appropriate places.

Do Alabamians love fried green tomatoes? "You bet 'cha." Just like other truly Southern dishes — grits and greens, notably — the fried green tomato has a place and taste all its own. If you've never eaten fried greens, try the recipe later in this book.

Stories abound about how the tomato, or "love apple" as it is sometimes called, got to the United States. Whether they arrived courtesy of African slaves, Italian immigrants, or some other unknown source -- arrive, they did -- and Southern cuisine is all the better for it. If you doubt the tomato's worth, try making gumbos, stews, soups, pasta sauces, barbecue sauces, and a bevy of other dishes without the inimitable tomato!

LYONNAISE CARROTS

2 small onions, minced
1/4 cup butter
1/2 teasp. salt

1/4 teasp. pepper
4 cups cooked carrots
1 tabsp. minced parsley

Brown onion in butter; add salt, pepper and carrots. Cover and cook slowly about 20 minutes. Sprinkle with parsley. Serves 8.

SHRIMP MADELINE

2 tabsp. dry mustard (English)
4 tabsp. butter
3 lbs. med. shrimp, uncooked

1/3 cup brandy
2 cups heavy cream
Salt and pepper to taste

Mix mustard with a small amount of water to make a light paste. Melt butter; sauté shrimp until water has evaporated. Pour brandy over pan; ignite. When flames subside, add the cream and cook, stirring constantly, until a smooth sauce forms. Add the mustard paste, salt and pepper to taste. Serve on a platter or in individual casserole dishes. Garnish with fresh parsley. Serves 8.

BREAST OF CHICKEN AND HAM SUPREME

3 chicken breasts, split
  and boned
1/2 lb. butter
6 slices ham, 1/4-inch thick
1 cup mushrooms
1 cup onions, sliced

3 cup chicken stock or broth
1-1/2 cups Half & Half
1/2 cup Sherry
1/2 cup Sherry
1/2 cup flour
1 cup uncooked brown rice

Melt butter in skillet, sauté until a light golden brown; salt to taste. Remove chicken to hot platter. Saute onions, remove from butter. Blend flour into butter until it is a smooth paste, then add chicken stock and cream, blend to deep smooth. Cook over low heat about five minutes. Place chicken on top of heated ham slices; top with sauce. Cook 20 minutes, serve over cooked rice.

SHRIMP SCAMPI

2 cloves garlic, minced
1 teasp. salt
1/4 teasp. black pepper
1/4 cup olive oil

2 lbs. shrimp, shelled and
 cleaned
2 tabsp. chopped parsley
Juice of 1 lemon

Combine garlic, salt, pepper, and oil. Arrange shrimp in single layer in broiler pan. Brush oil mixture over shrimp. Let stand about one hour to blend flavors. Broil shrimp slowly, turning once every five minutes or so until cooked. Sprinkle with parsley and lemon juice. Serves 4 – 6.

CRABE POINT CLEAR

1-1/2 cups mushrooms,
 quartered
1 tabsp. chopped shallots
4 tabsp. butter
5 tabsp. all-purpose flour
Dash thyme, dried and crushed
1 cup light cream

1/2 cup dry white wine
Salt, White pepper
Cayene pepper to taste
8 oz. fresh or frozen crab meat
Grated Parmesan cheese

In large saucepan, cook mushrooms and shallots in butter until tender. Blend in flour and thyme. Stir in cream; cook and stir until thickened and bubbly. Add wine. Season to taste with salt, pepper and cayenne. Stir in crab meat. Spoon into ramekins, then sprinkle with Parmesan cheese. Bake in 400° F. oven for about 15 minutes, or until crab is done and top is lightly browned. Serves 6.

SOLE DAUPHINE

1/2 cup dry vermouth	1-1/2 cups soft bread crumbs
4 tabsp. butter, melted	2 tabsp. butter, melted
4 teasp. chopped shallots	6 sole fillets (1-1/2 lbs)
1 tabsp. snipped parsley	1/2 teasp. lemon juice
1/2 teasp. dried tarragon, crushed	

Combine vermouth, four tablespoons melted butter, shallots, parsley and tarragon in a 13x9x2-inch baking dish; spread evenly in dish. Combine bread crumbs and remaining melted butter. Sprinkle over fish. Place fish, crumb side up, atop butter mixture. Bake in 425° F. oven for about 15 minutes, or until fish flakes easily with fork. Place fillets on serving plates. Strain juices. Stir in lemon juice; pour over each serving of fish. Serves 6.

STEAK FLAMBE'

4 (6 oz.) pieces sirloin steak, 1 inch thick	1/2 cup whipping cream
6 tabsp. butter	3 tabsp. Dijon mustard
Salt	2 tabsp. dairy sour cream
Pepper	1 teasp. Worcesterhire sauce
1/4 cup brandy	

Pound steak pieces to one-half inch thickness. In large skillet, heat butter and sauté sirloins for two minutes. Turn; season with salt and pepper. Cook to desired doneness, about two minutes each side for rare. Pour brandy over steaks; ignite. When flame dies, transfer steaks to warm serving platter.

Add whipping cream, mustard, sour cream, and Worcestershire sauce to juices in pan. Cook and stir until heated through. Pour sauce over steaks to serve. Serves 4.

FYI...Alabama's own Sister Schubert has a recipe for success: "Never compromise the ingredients." Her company never uses additives or preservatives. Patrica Schubert Barnes began making rolls in her own kitchen and now they're favored across the South.

Sister's product line includes Cranberry Nut Bread, Southern Cornbread and a wide variety of sweet rolls as well as dinner rolls. Today, her bakery turns out more than one million rolls per day!

CHICKEN BREASTS IN WHITE WINE

8 chicken breasts
4 tabsp. butter
1/2 cup white wine
Salt and pepper to taste

2 cups white sauce
1 can mushroom soup
1 cup sliced mushrooms, small
1/2 cup slivered almonds,
    toasted

Saute chicken breasts in butter until they are lightly browned. Arrange in bottom of casserole. Add wine, seasoning, mushroom soup and mushrooms to white sauce; pour over chicken. Bake at 350° F. for one hour. Ten minutes before removing from oven, sprinkle with almonds. Serves 8.

MARINATED EYE OF ROUND

1 (3 lb.) eye of round roast
Zesty Italian salad dressing

Crushed black pepper

Marinate roast in salad dressing for six hours or overnight. Remove from refrigerator; bring to room temperature. Preheat oven to 500° F. Cover roast with crushed black pepper; cook five minutes per pound. Turn oven off. Do not open oven door for two hours. Roast will be seared on the outside and pink on the inside.

CHESS CAKE

1 cup butter
1 lb. light brown sugar
1/2 cup granulated sugar
4 eggs, beaten

2 cups flour, sifted
1 teasp. baking powder
1 cup chopped pecans
1 teasp. vanilla extract

Preheat oven to 300° F. Heat butter and sugar; add other ingredients in order given. Bake in greased and floured pan (9x13x2) for 40 to 50 minutes. Cool ten minutes; cut into squares. May sprinkle with powdered sugar or serve with vanilla ice cream and caramel sauce. Serves 18.

Lemon Torte with Strawberries.
Photo courtesy of Alabama
Bureau of Tourism and Travel.

EASY COCONUT CAKE

1 box white pudding cake mix
1-1/4 cups sugar
1 cup milk

1 (6 oz.) pkg. frozen coconut
1 (9 oz.) carton frozen whipped
topping (Cool Whip)

According to package directions, mix and bake cake. While cake is baking, bring sugar and milk to boil. Punch holes in warm cake and pour warm mixture over. Refrigerate eight hours. Just before serving, spread cake with Cool Whip; sprinkle with coconut. Keep refrigerated.

STRAWBERRY CAKE

Add these ingredients:

1 box yellow cake mix
1 box strawberry jello
2/3 cup oil
4 eggs

2 tabsp. sugar
1/2 cup water
1/2 cup strawberries, sliced

Makes three layers.

Ice cake with these combined ingredients:

1 box powdered sugar, 3 tabsp. butter, 1/2 cup sliced strawberries. Delicious!

AMARETTO FREEZE

1/2 gallon vanilla ice cream,
softened
1 (6 oz.) carton Cool Whip

1/4 cup Amaretto
4 or 5 crushed Heath bars

Combine ice cream with Cool Whip and Amaretto. Spoon into parfait glasses, layering with crushed Heath bars. Freeze until set. Top with Cool Whip and more chopped Heath bars. Serves 6.

BUTTERMILK COCONUT PIE

5 eggs
1 stick butter
3/4 cup buttermilk

2 cups sugar
1 cup coconut
9 inch pie shell

Mix all ingredients. Pour into pie shell. Bake at 350° F. about 30 minutes, or until pie is done.

DID YOU KNOW...

- George Washington Carver's impressive agricultural experiments are exhibited at the Tuskegee Institute, where you will learn more about the dedicated educator, Booker T. Washington and his family home, The Oaks. The home was built by students and faculty, using bricks made by students, in 1899.

- Tuskegee Institute National Historic Site offers an important look at the contributions of African-American educators. Nearby is the Tuskegee Airmen National Historic Site, which honors the African-American airmen who served valiantly in World War II.

- More than 6,100 German POW's were once incarcerated in the little town of Aliceville. The Aliceville Museum now has displays of the era.

- Located between Tuscaloosa and Bessemer, at Vance, the Mercedes-Benz Visitor Center and Museum has a gift shop, plant tour by reservation, and Mercedes vehicles on display. This is the only Mercedes plant outside of Germany.

- Alabama's homegrown muscadines are known to make excellent grape juice, a product high in antioxidants.

Alabama Produce Stand.
Photo courtesy of Alabama Bureau of Tourism and Travel.

SERIOUSLY SEEKING ANTIQUES
AND FINDING COLLECTIBLE TREASURES

There are three types of antique shoppers. One type invites a couple of friends to hit the highways and byways in the SUV, road tripping around the region, having a grand time looking for quality antiques or collectibles but not having a particular piece in mind. They view their expedition as a treasure hunt where pot luck prevails. If they're lucky, they stumble upon something of superior workmanship that has withstood the test of time. If there's room in the SUV, they buy it and take it home, hoping to find the perfect spot to accommodate the prize.

More serious antique shoppers take luck out of the equation. They know what they want and they know how to research and find it. Usually a couple, they seldom shop with friends, and they often pull a small trailer behind the SUV. They know of a couple of places to ferret out the object of their desire because they've planned in advance. One of the best places to research is the Internet. Those who aren't savvy to the technology have perhaps spent years developing relationships with top dealers and auctioneers who help them find the item they seek. That's good, too.

And then there's the third type. Those who enjoy the chase; who go into a shop or mall because they like the way it looks. They also visit fleas and even garage sales, because sometimes, great finds are waiting. This type remembers hearing stories of astute collectors who found a $5 item at an antique mall and sold the rare small piece for thousands at Sotheby's. Could an old piece of ornate porcelain really be a rare, 175-year old piece from Paris?

The South is one of the best places to be for antique collectors. The selection is still good, and the prices are far more reasonable than in major cities north of the Mason Dixon line. If important antiques are on your list, head for New Orleans, the South's premier place to shop for antiques and one of the nation's best. You'll find enough quality antique shops on Magazine Street to furnish a small town of marvelous old mansions. And if you want more, Royal Street is flush with antique shops and upscale galleries. Both Magazine and Royal Streets are in the French Quarter, as are countless shops and galleries.

Though there are entirely too many fine shops to include in one article, I will mention a few that are particularly interesting to me because they sell quality antiques and *objets d'art* and/or they've been around a long time.

One of the oldest is Waldhorn and Adler on Royal Street. This shop has occupied the same location since 1881, and then there's MS Rau where serious collectors have found important 18th century English and French antiques since 1912. Three generations have operated the French Antique Shop on Royal, which began about 100 years ago when ancestors came to New Orleans from Paris. Expect fine European things and an excellent selection of antique lighting.

Ida Manheim Antiques on Royal has a history that began in 1919 when her grandfather came here from Austria. He was a master cabinet maker who quickly built a clientele. His son became a legendary dealer of fine antiques, and now Ida has the reputation as someone who knows all aspects of the business. Select from the Continent at Maison de Provence, where France, Italy and Germany are well represented in furniture and decorative arts. These shops are a few of many. Some sell antique silver and jewelry exclusively, so ask around or look on the net.

If your taste runs to the lighter side, try Vintage 429 or Jezebel's Art and Antiques, both in the Quarter. With designers looking for good architectural salvage, there's Armadillo South on Washington Avenue, where good originals and great reproductions are plentiful.

Elsewhere in Louisiana, Fireside Antiques in Baton Rouge has a huge selection of French formal pieces. This shop is well known throughout the South, for good reason.

Washington, Louisiana, boasts an old school house now being utilized as an antiques mall for about 100 dealers. It's aptly named Old Schoolhouse Antique Mall. This town, founded in 1720, calls itself the antique capital of Acadiana. You'll find interesting shops in Lafayette and throughout this region, so plan to spend a few days here.

Shreveport has quality dealers and fun fleas, with a few good malls for balance. East on Interstate 20, head toward Monroe and don't miss Antique Alley in West Monroe's Cotton Port Historic District. This antique shoppers delight offers a big antique mall, individual shops, a tea room, specialty shops and a B&B. About 100 dealers are here selling formal antiques, old things and collectibles.

Natchez is one of Mississippi's premier antique towns where 18 dealers sell high quality antiques. Many of the shops are on Franklin Street, known as "Antique Row." Natchez is a unique and memorable place where antebellum mansions reign supreme in the South, so plan a few days here.

The Mississippi Gulf Coast towns of Biloxi, Gulfport and Bay St. Louis have about 26 dealers and a few malls.

Jackson's 33 dealers offer a variety of furniture and decorative arts. Start at the old Fondren-Woodland Hills suburb where the new focus is on antiques. Shop at St. Martin's Gallery for exciting French and English antiques. Many items here came directly from France's Provence region. The Antique Market on State Street is a mall, but a mall selling antiques only. Containers are shipped from England and Wales. East of Jackson, the new Antique Galleria is open in Collins. Celebrity dealers Delta Burke and husband Gerald McRaney, a Collins native, are involved. It's located at the intersection of Highways 49 and 84.

In the Delta, Lina's Interiors is an institution on Greenville; it's a favorite of decorators and collectors. In Greenwood, Heritage House Antiques sells English pieces and others, too, including some American primitives. Several dealers are located in this region, so look around.

Meridian, with its 12 shops, plus Columbus and Tupelo have enough shops and malls to keep collectors busy. West Point has Annabelle's, which offers a good selection, as well as another mall. The picture perfect town of Oxford has eight dealers of antiques and attic finds.

Alabama's Gulf Coast touts the Daphne Antique Galleria as the largest mall of the Eastern Shore of Mobile Bay. Expect to find more than 175 dealers covering 27,000 square feet under one roof. The towns of Fairhope and Foley have nice offerings, too. Mobile has a couple of good malls, including Cotton City's good mix of antiques and smalls. It's an old

44

theater building.

Birmingham's Riverchase Antiques Gallery and several shops in Mountain Brook make for a good day of shopping. Check out the Five Points area, too.

North of Birmingham, Cullman's Southern Accents Architectural Antiques, Inc. is in the National Historic District. This place offers architectural antiques of all kinds – even hardware—iron fencing, statuary, bathroom fixtures, garden accents, and more.

Historic Opelika is home to Angel's Antique and Flea Market. With 300 dealers at 65,000 square feet, it's one of the region's newest and largest malls. Also in Opelika, find Courthouse Square Antique Mall and Shops. This one's a cut above.

Head toward the north Alabama mountains and find Mentone, a small town known for summer camps. White Elephant Antiques is in a turn of the century Victorian structure built in Mentone's heyday. Rooms at the antique shop are filled with old things and collectibles.

There are hundreds of outstanding antique shops and malls in the three-state area and we would like to have mentioned each one. Find out more through these publications: *Antiques Gazette* (the antiquesgazette.com); *Southeastern Antiquing and Collecting Magazine* (antiquing@go-star.com); or *Mississippi Antiques* at 888.327.3332. Most dealers have these publications and they are free to customers.

MOUNTAIN TOP FLEA MARKET
And More Great Finds

Everybody loves a flea...and Mountain Top is the biggest in Alabama and one of the biggest in the county! It's in a lovely spot at the foothills of Sand Mountain, six miles west of Attalla on Hwy. 278. If you're north of Birmingham on I-59, you're within seven miles of this shopper's paradise. There is definitely something for everyone somewhere within the 2.6 (that's 2 and 6/10) miles of shopping pleasure, where more than 1,500 dealers have displayed their wares. Find the most unimaginable merchandise, from old farm implements to new power tools; from old furniture and antique smalls to new furniture; also find clothes, accessories, books and bargains!

Mountain Top Flea Market is open one day each week year 'round, from 5:00 a.m. TIL each Sunday, rain or shine, and it is well worth the drive if you're anywhere in the South. This flea has been rated # 1 in the Fairs and Flea Market category by the Alabama Bureau of Tourism and Travel. It is also in the Top 50 Flea Markets in the nation, which is one good reason that this site has attracted more than 1.64 million visitors!

Many shoppers make it a day, beginning with breakfast foods sold at the main concession and other foods at other concessions throughout the day. The barbecue and home-made ice cream venues are among the most popular.

See more at Mountain Tops web site: www.lesdeal.com or call 800.535.2286.

Elsewhere in the vicinity, take a look at "Antique Attalla" in downtown Attalla, where there are three blocks of antique shops and specialty stores. About 21 shops offer interesting items. Head northwest of Attalla, and not too far away find the Unclaimed Baggage Center at Scottsboro, a massive building filled with unclaimed merchandise. It's been featured on Oprah, The Today Show, and David Letterman. Visit at 509 W. Willow Street Monday through Saturday, and see about 7000 new items arriving daily. For information, see www.unclaimedbaggage.com or call 256.259.1525.

OF MULES AND MEN...

DO NOT BECOME EMOTIONAL OVER A
MULE WHEN A THOROUGHBRED
IS WAITING IN THE STALL.

KEEP PLENTY OF GOOD HAY IN THE BARN
AND YOU'LL SEE THAT A SMART HORSE
NEVER FORGETS THE WAY HOME.

IF YOU'RE LOOKING FOR A QUALITY STALLION...
DON'T GO NEAR THE DONKEY CORRAL.

WISE WOMEN KNOW...

STRENGTH MAY BE THE CHARM OF A MAN,
BUT CHARM IS THE STRENGTH OF A WOMAN.

EVEN IF YOU'RE ON THE RIGHT TRACK...
A TRAIN WILL RUN OVER YOU IF YOU STOP MOVING.

NOTHING HAPPENS BY ACCIDENT. IN EVERY
STRUGGLE THERE IS A BLESSING.

47

LOUISIANA

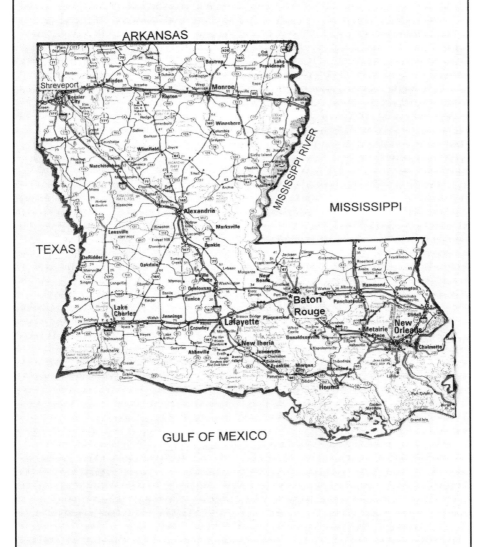

ARKANSAS

TEXAS

MISSISSIPPI

GULF OF MEXICO

LOUISIANA FACTS

- The world's largest heliport is located in Morgan City.

- Louisiana hosts more than 600 festivals each year.

- Sci-Port Discovery in Shreveport is 67,000 square feet of excitement in a hand-on children's science museum.

- Orleans Parish is the lowest point in Louisiana, five feet below sea level.

- The oldest city in the Louisiana Purchase is Natchitoches, founded in 1714.

- Southern University is the largest predominantly black university in the nation.

- Louisiana was named by French explorer Robert de LaSalle for Louis XIV, King of France.

- The nation's first opera was performed in New Orleans in 1796.

- New Orleans native Daniel Louis "Satchmo" Armstrong is credited with making jazz popular worldwide.

- Singer/actor Harry Connick, Jr., is the son of long-time New Orleans District Attorney Harry Connick, Sr.

- America's oldest rice mill is located in New Iberia at Konriko Company.

- Steen's Syrup Mill in Abbeville is the world's largest producer of sugarcane syrup.

- Mulate's Cajun Restaurant in Breaux Bridge has withstood more than five generations of waltzing and two-stepping on the original dance floor.

- Bayou Folk Museum in Cloutierville depicts pioneer life in Cane River Country and the memorabilia of *avante garde* writer Kate Chopin.

- Louisiana has two cuisines, similar but distinct. Creole, which has a bit of an Italian influence and uses a tomato base, and Cajun, which begins many recipes with a brown roux (gravy).

- The French Quarter's Pontalba Buildings flank Jackson Square on either side. They are block-long, re-bricked buildings constructed by Baroness Micaela de Pontalba on land inherited from her father. The outstanding cast-iron railings of the former row townhouses contain "AP" which stands for Almonester and Pontalba.

LOUISIANA

INTRODUCTION

Louisiana is a state whose diversity is so great it could be two states in one: North Louisiana and South Louisiana. The northern part of the state is more like Dallas than New Orleans. Next to the cities down south, this region is conservative with a large Protestant base. South Louisiana is primarily Catholic, playful, and forever ready for a party. And to the legions of people who love the great state of Louisiana, the cultural differences are part of the appeal, and so are the 600 or so annual festivals that commemorate the rich culture.

It is unimaginable but true that in 1803, the Louisiana Territories were bought for about four cents an acre. That "Louisiana Purchase" included what was later to become thirteen states, though the name was retained for one state, Louisiana. The purchase, engineered by Napoleon, doubled the size of the United States and gave it a global importance, a fact not overlooked by U.S. President Thomas Jefferson.

In its glorious past, Louisiana was home to native Americans whose massive mounds at Poverty Point State Historic area near Epps indicate that it was the site of civilization circa 1500 BC. Later, Spain ruled the region and the Spanish influence is still seen in the decorative ironwork and architecture. Spanish conquistadors came to the new land as early as 1519.

And then came the colorful Cajuns – "Cajun" being a word derived from Acadian people who were exiled from Acadia (Nova Scotia) in the mid 1700s. The people were French Catholics who came from France to Nova Scotia around 1605. They lived in peace with the Indian tribes, but the story changed when France ceded Acadia to Great Britain in 1713. The migration from Acadia continued until 1755, by then about 1600 Acadians had left Nova Scotia and headed to the bayous and wetlands of the South. They formed communities and built churches, obtained land grants, raised cattle, grew cotton, and hunted, fished and trapped to feed their growing families. Finally, the Cajuns lived in peace and relative isolation along the bayous – those people with the surnames of LeBlanc, Pitre, Robicheaux, Mouton, Breaux, Broussard, Cormier, Delahoussaye, and others. They spoke their native French and used fish and game to create their delicious, spicy food, which is still much in demand today.

Back in the 1800s, African Americans perhaps enjoyed a better life here than in other places in the South. "Free People of Color" owned property and later had their own universities, among then Xavier, Dillard, Southern and Grambling.

In the 1900s, the peaceful, God-fearing and fun loving Cajuns were about to encounter discrimination that had nothing to do with skin colo but rather education and language. Learning about life and survival skills on the bayou was no longer enough. Under the administration of Governor Huey P. Long, formal education became mandatory and Acadian children had problems; they did not speak English and teachers did not teach in French. Unfortunately, for many years, some of the teachers punished Cajun children for speaking the only language they knew. Gradually, the rich Cajun culture was recognized and Cajun pride came to the forefront.

The Council for the Development of French in Louisiana (CODOFIL) was organized in 1968 and served as a catalyst of sorts for a French renaissance. CODOFIL became a state agency designed to preserve and promote Louisiana's French language, heritage and culture. And what a proud heritage it is! Cajun food and music have enjoyed a popularity that reaches across the USA and Europe. *Laissez le bon temps rouler* – let the good times roll – is a rallying call for Cajuns and all those who want to be, including this writer who had the good fortune to live in Louisiana for years.

Remember that what other states call counties are known as "parishes" in Louisiana. If someone says "Caddo County" instead of Caddo Parish, they are surely outsiders. And yes, there is a distinct difference in 'Cajun' and 'Creole.' Cajuns, we know, are part of a culture that sprang primarily from the traditions of France and Nova Scotia, but later melded with Native American, Spanish, English and German. Creole refers to those born in the colony before the Louisiana Purchase. Creoles enjoyed a blending of French, Spanish, African or Caribbean cultures and settled mostly in cities, such as New Orleans, whereas Cajuns preferred the privacy and peace of the bayous. The difference in food is that Creole cuisine is generally tomato-based while Cajun is roux-based. In Cajun households, the rule is "first you make a roux." See how to make a roux in the food section at the end of this chapter.

Old State Capitol, Baton Rouge.
Photo courtesy of Louisiana Office of Tourism.

North Louisiana

Shreveport

Shreveport is a terrific city and the heart of the region known as the Ark-La-Tex because of its location in the upper northwest corner near the states of Texas and Arkansas. Near downtown, glitzy gaming casinos on the Red River and their adjoining hotels offer a lifestyle similar to Las Vegas, while at the other end of Texas Street sits the big First Methodist Church. It appears to watch over the heart of downtown Shreveport with grace and grandeur.

A culturally rich city, Shreveport offers the Symphony Orchestra, the Opera, Community Theatre, The Stand Theatre (renovated around1925) , the R.W. Norton Art Gallery, the Meadows Museum of Art, the Spring Street Museum, the Pioneer Heritage Center, to name a few of the cultural offerings. Nature lovers flock to the parks, lakes, outdoor events, golf, tennis, and team sports. There's Fairfield Historic District, known for lovely old homes, great restaurants, the American Rose Center — where more than 20,000 rose bushes bloom in about 60 gardens — and it's also the headquarters of the American Rose Society.

American Rose Center Chapel, Shreveport.
Photo courtsey of Betty Jo LeBrun,
Shreveport-Bossier Film Office.

The prestigious Centenary College is based in Shreveport, also the LSU Medical Center and the Shreveport campus of LSU. Sports fans appreciate the Shreveport Captains (professional baseball) and the outstanding bass fishing at nearby Toledo Bend. Lake Bistineau, Caddo Lake and Cross Lake are hot fishing and boating spots, too. Pari-mutuel betting is available at the big Louisiana Downs, and then there are the casinos! Fun festivals include the Red River Revel, the largest annual arts events in North Louisiana. Holiday in Dixie in mid-April remains a popular event; it's a top 100 in the nation, according to the American Bus Association.

The Red River divides Shreveport and **Bossier City** (say Boz-yer), and now, across the Texas Street Bridge over the Red River into Bossier, find the new Louisiana Boardwalk, a $150 million-plus development on 50 acres along the waterfront. It's an up-market shoppers delight that invites strollers to visit boutiques, restaurants, galleries, clubs, theaters and more.

At Barksdale Air Force Base, the Eighth Air Force Museum features exhibits from WWII to the present. At Bossier City's East Bank Gallery, see rotating exhibits of regional/international artists. Also in the Bossier vicinity, music fans from pre-1960 may remember the Louisiana Hayride, a radio program and venue that gave a start to such luminaries as Elvis Presley and Hank Williams. Elvis appeared live at the Hayride in the early 1950s. Perhaps it's where he perfected his style.

Leave the Ark-La-Tex and head toward **Arcadia**, where the notorious Bonnie Parker and Clyde Barrow met their demise after robbing many banks during the Depression. Next town is **Ruston**, home of Louisiana Tech and the Military Museum, where 7,000 artifacts chart a century of wars. Kids love the IDEA Place on the Tech campus. They discover science in a hands-on environment.

MONROE

Monroe and West Monroe, the cities on the Quachita River, are the sprawling trade centers for this part of the state, and the Quachita (say Wa-she-taw) is one of the prettiest rivers around. Antiques are still plentiful here, and not too pricey.

In case you didn't know, Delta Airlines got its inauspicious start as a crop dusting company flying small planes over the crops of the rich Delta land in the region. Learn more about the history of this aviation pioneer at the Aviation and Military Museum of Louisiana, Inc. Another well-known product name here is Coca-Cola, first bottled by Monroe's Joseph Biedenharn. The Biedenharn Museum and Garden features the Biedenharn home, the Bible Museum, and the ELsong Garden and Conservatory.

Another garden to see is the Louisiana Purchase Gardens and Zoo in Monroe, an 82-acre natural habitat for exotic animals. Train and boat rides are available at this fun and educational outing for the family. The Black Bayou Lake offers fishing, canoeing, bird-watching, an observation tower and boat launch.

While in North Louisiana, don't miss the opportunity to see the area's small towns, among them **Minden**, near the scenic Lake Bistineau and Caney Lake. Saturday nights from February through October, Champion Park Speedway offers the excitement of dirt-track racing. **Mooringsport** is proud of the pretty Caddo Lake and the last surviving vertical-lift bridge. The 1914 bridge is listed on the National Register of Historic Places. **Mansfield**, site of a major Civil War battle, now has a museum exhibiting Civil War artifacts. **Bastrop**, the number five-ranked duck hunting site in the country, also offers a National Wildlife Refuge and Nature Preserve.

CENTRAL LOUISIANA

NATCHITOCHES

This part of Louisiana is the most difficult to characterize because it's not exactly Cajun or Creole, but a wonderfully versatile region known as "the Crossroads." If you saw the movie *Steel Magnolias*, you saw Natchitoches (say Nak-a-tish), the lovely town on the Cane River. Written by native Robert Harling, it was only natural to film *Steel Magnolias* in the town that influenced the book. Some of the locals rented their homes to the movie actors and crew, which still makes for interesting conversation. Several tours of filming sites are available.

Natchitoches is also the oldest settlement in the Louisiana Purchase. It was founded in 1714, four years before New Orleans. Natchitoches, not to be confused with Nagodoches, Texas, boasts a downtown main street where shops and restaurants line the west side of the Cane River, and a park-like setting runs beside the river. The town also boasts a 33-block historic district designated a National Historic Landmark, a prestigious honor indeed. About 17,000 people call Natchitoches home.

Yucca House on Melrose Plantation. Photo courtesy of Louisiana Office of Tourism.

Near Natchitoches in the Cane River National Heritage area are two National Historic Landmarks that should be on every itinerary: Melrose and the Kate Chopin House. The plantation complex of Melrose (c. 1796) was built by former slave Marie-Therese Coincoin, who had four children fathered by a slave and ten children of Franco-African blood fathered by a Frenchman and plantation owner named Thomas Pierre Metoyer, who later freed Coincoin's children. The first house at Melrose, Yucca, was built in 1796 when Marie-Therese was 54. Coincoin and her sons got land grants, worked the fields and grew the plantation to 6,000 acres. By the 1830s, Melrose is said to have encompassed more than 10,000 acres. Slave labor was used to work the plantation and construct the other buildings, among them Africa House, built in 1800 and the main house, built in 1833.

The tough economic times of the 1840s brought new ownership, Henry and Hypolite Hertzog, who, in turn, lost it after the Civil

War. In 1884, Melrose was acquired by Joseph Henry. At the turn of the century, it became the home of Jason and "Miss Cammie" Henry, who were arts aficionados and most interested in historic preservation.

Mrs. Henry invited artists and writers to come to Melrose for unlimited visits. Among those who came were Erskine Caldwell, Gwen Briscoe, Alberta Kinsey and Lyle Saxon. One friend and collaborator of Mrs. Henry was Francois Mignon, who came for a six-week visit and stayed for 32 years! During this time, a one-time cook at Melrose, Clementine Hunter, emerged as a celebrated primitive artist. She later said that she painted because "art was all around her." She lived at Melrose most of her life. The house is open for tours and is well worth seeing. It is 16 miles south of Natchitoches.

Early feminist writer Kate Chopin created a stir in her actions and her literature back in the day. Her story of a woman's search for fulfillment, *The Awakening,* is considered a classic in feminist literature and it was written in 1898. The Kate Chopin Home, a National Historic Landmark near **Cloutierville**, is open for tours. See other antebellum tour homes along the Cane River and the Red River; contact numbers are near the back of this book.

ALEXANDRIA

Alexandria is the largest and busiest town in the central Louisiana Crossroads region. It is home to about 50,000 people, but Alex lacks the pre-Civil War history prominent in other parts of the state. Unfortunately, the town was invaded and burned by Union troops in 1864. Kent House, built between 1796 and 1800, is one

Kent House Plantation, Alexandria.
Photo courtesy of Louisiana Office of Tourism.

local plantation that was spared. The house and gardens have been restored to former grandeur and are open for tours.

The pretty river town of Alexandria has a good zoo and art museum and once boasted the Hotel Bentley, long a grand and favorite hotel whose guests included Dwight Eisenhower, Gen. George Patton, and actors, among them John Wayne. This hotel was called "The Biltmore of the Bayou." So sorry it is now closed.

Grand lobby of the Hotel Bentley, once an Alexandria showplace. Photo courtesy of Louisiana Office of Tourism.

Hodges Gardens, Many. Photo courtesy of Louisiana Office of Tourism.

Natural beauty abounds here, with the Dewey Mills Wildlife Management Area, Kincaid Lake, and the Wild Azalea National Recreation Trail. Also in central Louisiana, fishermen flock to the 185,000-acre Toledo Bend Reservoir, while gardeners seek out the outstanding Hodges Gardens, a multi-level showplace complete with waterfalls.

Visitors should take advantage of the many small towns in this region, including **Winnfield**, home of three Louisiana governors including Earl K. Long, who had a tumultuous liaison with the stripper Blaze Star. Other interesting small towns in the region include **Many** (say MAN-ee), **Leesville**, home of the U.S. Army's Fort Polk, and **DeRidder**, where the Lois Loftin Doll Museum is housed in the historic train depot, where more than 3,000 dolls are displayed.

DID YOU KNOW?

- Louisiana's 6.5 million acres of wetlands are vitally important to the region's ecological system.
- The oldest city in the Louisiana Purchase is Natchitoches, founded in 1714.

South Louisiana

And here we are in the land of *joie de vivre*, Cajun Country! What a place! Not only is South Louisiana home to this country's number one party town, New Orleans, but it's also where the ragin' Cajuns let the good times roll. Weekends mean one continuous party in Cajun country – whether it's one or more of the many festivals, a *fais do-do* somewhere in the community, or a gathering of friends to cook up seafood in the outdoor kitchen – the people here pass a good time, cher! The good times are usually on weekends, for during the week, Cajuns work hard. "Work hard, play hard" is a part of their philosophy, and they do both well.

The Legend of Evangeline

In South Louisiana, there's an air of romance that began with Henry Wadsworth Longfellow's poem, *Evangeline*. Legend has it that Evangeline and her intended, Gabriel, were separated during the Acadian exile. Evangeline waited faithfully for Gabriel to find her. The story is that they finally met under the "Evangeline Oak" in St. Martinville many years after they left Nova Scotia. It was here that Gabriel told his former fiancée that he thought he'd lost her forever and married another. According to legend, Evangeline soon died of a broken heart. That's one version of the story. Another says that Evangeline became a nun in Philadelphia and while working at a hospital, saw Gabriel, by then an old man, on his deathbed; she died shortly thereafter. Rumor has it that when Longfellow wrote the poem in 1847, he loosely based his poem on fact, but the fact is that his facts were less than accurate, some say.

There appears to be a continuing debate about the young lovers. Yet another story, *Acadian Reminiscences: The True Story of Evangeline*, which is probably more accurate, was published in 1907 by Judge Felix Voorhies. He said that his grandmother told him the story of Emmeline Labiche and her lost love, Louis Arceneaux, and how, after many years, they were reunited. Whatever the true story of the star-crossed lovers, it makes an interesting recollection. Another more current version is *In Search of Evangeline – Birth and Evolution of the Evangeline Myth*, by Carl A. Brasseaux. Surely after reading all the available material, one will form their own conclusion.

Lafayette

Since we're already talking about Cajuns and the 22 parishes that make up Cajun Country, also called Acadiana, we'll start in Lafayette, the heart of Acadiana. This city of 110,500 or so is often surprising to outsiders. Some arrive expecting to find swamps and pirogues and alligators. They will, within fairly close proximity of Lafayette, but Lafayette proper has a flair and sophistication all its own. There's an abundance of world-class restaurants, smart shopping, savvy people, lovely homes, a university, and local residents who care enough to participate in the community. A previous article in a regional publication said: "In Lafayette the seafood is fresher, the sauces spicer, the music livelier and the heritage richer."

Luckily, the fascinating French culture is still alive and well in laid-back Lafayette. Even the oil-rich economy of a few years back didn't do much to alter the *joie de vivre* for which the region is known. Before oil was discovered, agriculture, cattle raising, hunting and trapping were the major sources of income. The history of Lafayette, originally called Vermilionville, is well depicted in two living history museums: Acadian Village and Vermillionville.

Acadian Village and Tropical Gardens, Lafayette.
Photo courtesy of Louisiana Office of Tourism.

Acadian Village is a recreated village of authentic Acadian houses and life styles of an early settlement, complete with costumed workers. Tours are conducted in English and French in this folk life museum of Acadian culture and heritage. Another look at Cajun/Creole heritage and folklife is Vermilionville, situated on 22 acres. This living history village recreates life on the bayou from 1765 to 1890. Costumed craftspeople demonstrate Cajun and zydeco music, cooking, crafts and more. There's also a nature trail, restaurant and gift shop. Both educational attractions serve as monuments to proud people, the Cajuns and the Creoles.

Food and music are what brings people to Lafayette and the surrounding communities, and sometimes both are available at one location. Zydeco is a revved-up version of Cajun music and has more black band members than white, whereas Cajun is primarily white and the lyrics are French. Don't miss the music of this region, for it is unique and wonderful. My personal favorite place to hear the music and savor the food is a superb restaurant in an old brick general store in **Breaux Bridge** — the Crawfish Capital of the world — about six miles from Lafayette. It is the Café des Amis, where sumptuous Saturday brunch is generally served to the music of a zydeco band.

Back in Lafayette, learn more about the region at the Alexandre Mouton House Museum. It's located in the house of Lafayette's founder, Jean Mouton, whose son was Governor Alexandre Mouton. For an even more authentic Cajun experience, take a trip into the Atchafalaya (say 'Chaf-a-lie-yah) Swamp with well-trained naturalists who tell about the environ-ment as well as the scenic beauty.

Evangeline Downs, just north of Lafayette, is where locals and visi-tors go for a good time. It's not Churchill Downs and the horses more than likely wouldn't win the Kentucky Derby, but it's fast-paced fun with a

Statue of Jean Mouton,
founder of Lafayette.
Photo courtesy of
Louisiana Office of Tourism.

local flavor. Once the track announcer says, "Ils sont partis!" (say 'ill-sont-partee', meaning 'off and running') the excitement begins. Lafayette and the nearby towns have so much to see and do, a few days are warranted to even scratch the surface of this Mecca for music aficionadoes who crave a certain ethnic sound.

The Atchafalaya Swamp near Henderson.
Photo courtesy of Louisiana Office of Tourism.

THE MUSIC OF THE PEOPLE

Saturday night is the time to find the people of Acadiana living large and practicing *joie de vivre*. In the small towns of the region, there are always one or two places where Cajuns gather to dance and "pass a good time, cher!" You hear the music before you find the place, for the unmistakable sound of this unique music, whether Cajun or zydeco, wafts over the flat land and lush mysterious bayous.

Cajun music is older than zydeco; some say it sounds like bluegrass with a French accent. This music came to South Louisiana with the Acadian exiles that left Nova Scotia with few musical instruments, but their love of music was intact. Upon arrival, they used the instruments they had, and then they made their own out of household items, such as spoons, washboards, and clacking sticks. With the fiddle and triangle as the principal instruments and the accordion introduced later, Cajun music is now a beloved art form that must be seen as well as heard. Seeing these fun-loving people dance the Cajun two-step, or chank-a-chank, to their own music is a true Cajun treat!

Zydeco is a new form of Cajun music. It evolved in the 1950s from regional music called "lala," a black Creole sound that originated in Southwest Louisiana, though it was influenced by Blues and Soul. The principal instruments are the *frotoir*, or metal rub-board, which is played with thimbles on the fingers or spoons in the hands, and the accordion.

The late Clifton Chenier became known as the "King of Zydeco." Zydeco music enjoyed a huge revival in the 1980s, and both Cajun and zydeco now draw thousands of people to festivals and dance halls throughout Acadiana. Two major festivals celebrate the music of the region; they are Festivals Acadiens in mid-September and Festival International de Louisiane in mid-April, both in Lafayette.

Allons à Lafayette!

LAKE CHARLES

Lake Charles is a city west of Lafayette near the Texas line. A very high bridge crosses the Calcasieu River and the lake that gives the town of about 70,000 its water sports opportunities. Campers and boaters are to be found at the Sam Houston Jones State Park located at the confluence of three rivers.

Boating at Sam Houston Jones State Park.
Photo courtesy of Louisiana Office of Tourism.

Nature lovers, there's a 180-mile drive through marshlands that provide a chance to see alligators, wildlife, migratory fowl and exotic birds. It's called the Creole Nature Trail, and it's a great place to find a perfect picnic spot.

Head back east on I-10 for the small towns of Acadiana that add so much to the culture: **Jennings**, **Crowley**, **Rayne**, and the towns north of I-10: **Ville Platte, Washington** – where a huge old school house has been converted to an antique mall – **Grand Coteau, Church Point, Eunice** and **Opelousas**. Eunice and Opelousas are good bets to find places to hear zydeco music. Ask the locals.

OPELOUSAS

Opelousas, Louisiana's third oldest city, is the home of the original Southwest Louisiana Zydeco Music Festival held each September. Clifton Chenier was born in Opelousas.

Though distinct music has been a part of Cajun culture for generations, the music is now popular outside the region. And yes, the good times roll! The revival continues today as thousands of new converts flock to Cajun music venues wherever they may be.

Near Opelousas, find the Academy of the Sacred Heart at Grand Coteau, the second oldest educational institution west of the Mississippi River. Sacred Heart is a girls' school dating back to 1821. A magnificent avenue of pines and moss-draped oaks serve as the entry to the academy and convent. This is the first of the international network of Sacred Heart Schools and the place where "The Miracle of Grand Coteau" occurred.

According to legend, young Mary Wilson arrived in 1866 in hopes of receiving the habit of the Sacred Heart Sisters. She was not well upon arrival and her illness progressed. She vomited blood several times a day, could not eat, had a high fever and was in constant pain. She had been given up for dead when the miracle came through the intercession of Blessed John Berchmans, a Jesuit seminarian who had died 250 years earlier. As Mary prayed for deliverance from her great pain, she heard a whisper and saw a figure standing by her bed. It was John Berchmans. She did as he said, and she was cured. The Mother and Sisters could not believe that the girl had come from her death bed well and free of pain. The Reverend Mother called in doctors who confirmed that the near-death girl was indeed well; they could not explain the transition by any ordinary natural laws. The Miracle of Grand Coteau was accepted as authentic, and in 1888, Pope Leo XIII canonized John Berchmans. Thus, Grand Coteau became the only U.S. miracle site recognized by the Vatican.

Nearby is the large and lovely Chretien Point Plantation, see opposite page, where the pirate Jean Lafitte is said to have brought his lady loves in the 1800s. It's now a popular B&B inn. Still in Acadiana south of I-10, great places to visit are **Kaplan**, **Abbeville**, **New Iberia** and **St. Martinville**. Kaplan is a treasure and pure Cajun in its demeanor; Abbeville is an interesting place on the bayou that boasts the Wetlands Acadian Cultural Center, restaurants that serve superb Cajun fare, and an enviable community theater.

Chretien Point Plantation.
Photo courtesy of Louisiana Office of Tourism.

New Iberia is where you'll find the exquisite antebellum home, Shadows on the Teche (c. 1830). It is owned and operated by the National Trust for Historic Preservation, the only NTHP property in Louisiana. Formerly the home of sugarcane planter David Weeks, Shadows borders the Bayou Teche and is surrounded by shady live oak trees loaded with gently swaying Spanish moss. Furnished in period antiques, the home is open for tours.

Shadows on the Teche, New Iberia.
Photo courtesy fo Louisiana Office of Tourism.

62

"Shadows" is a remarkable example of the authentic historic homes still available in the South. South of New Iberia is Cypremort Point, called by locals "The Cajun Riviera." Long piers over the bay are good for sunbathing, fishing, and watching sunsets. Along with private homes and camps, Cypremort Point State Park is here. Don't miss the towns of **Jeanerette**, **Franklin** and **Morgan City**, also south of New Iberia. Avery Island's Jungle Gardens and the Tabasco Country Store and Visitors Center are in the vicinity, and so is Rip Van Winkle Gardens, a National Historic Landmark on Jefferson Island.

You're now near St. Martinville, the place where exiled aristocrats from France began settling along the Bayou Teche before the Acadians from Nova Scotia arrived. Even the local dialect is somewhat different here than that of neighboring communities. Find the Evangeline Oak, made famous as the legendary meeting place of Evangeline and Gabriel. It still thrives at the Bayou Teche landing in town. The statue of Evangeline, made in the likeness of the late actress Delores Del Rio, can be seen at the historic Saint Martin de Tours Catholic Church, founded around 1765. The current church building was begun by slave labor in 1832.

Evangeline Statue, St. Martinville.
Photo courtesy of
Louisiana Office of Tourism.

To see an authentic Cajun "raised cottage," visit the Longfellow-Evangeline State Historic Site in St. Martinville. Interpreters tell about life on an 1800s bayou plantation. From here, find your way to **Breaux Bridge** on the Bayou Teche, home of the Crawfish Festival, the original Mulate's Cajun Restaurant, and Lake Martin, where alligators can be seen sunning on the bank. From here, head on out to I-10 and cross the Atchafalaya Basin to Baton Rouge.

BATON ROUGE

Baton Rouge, the state capital, has been a hotbed for political shenanigans, from the Long family dynasty to the colorful Cajun former governor Edwin Edwards, who appeared to delight in courting scandal. Today it's a thriving new South city, relatively free of the politics of smoke-filled rooms. About 228,000 people live here.

Legend has it that when Frenchman Pierre le Moyne, sieur d'Iberville, came up the Mississippi River in 1699, he saw an unusual sight: a tall cypress pole coated with the red blood of animals. The red stick marked the hunting ground of the two Indian tribes that

62

shared the area. Shortly thereafter, the name "Baton Rouge" the French words for "red stick," took hold.

Once known as the "Florida Parishes" because Britain was ceded the area known as West Florida in 1763, Baton Rouge maintained its French character. In 1779, the Spanish captured the British fortification and flew the Spanish flag for 20 years. The region again passed to the French just before the Louisiana Purchase in 1803, and then Baton Rouge came into its own after having flown the flags of seven nations.

The Old State Capitol, built of cast iron and brick in 1849, looks like an impenetrable fortress with its crenelated exterior. The restored interior of this Gothic Revival structures features a circular iron staircase reaching up to the stained-glass rotunda. It now houses the Louisiana Center for Political and Governmental History. Tours of this architecturally significant building are available.

The New State Capitol was built in 1932 under the administration of Governor Huey P. Long. The 34-story (450 feet) structure, Art Deco-style, is the tallest state capitol. At construction, it was the tallest building in the South and the observation deck on the 27th floor offers a spectacular view of the city. The Old Governor's Mansion, also built by Huey P. Long in 1930 to rival the White House in Washington, has been restored and is open for tours.

The sophisticated Louisiana Art and Science Museum's $16 million Irene W. Pennington Planetarium is open downtown and it is indeed one of the world's top multimedia presentations. The plane-

The Old Governor's Mansion now houses the Foundation for Historical Louisiana.
Photo courtesy of Louisiana Office of Tourism.

64

64

tarium programs promise a new universe of sight and sound, nothing short of amazing. Even better, there's a new trolley service operating downtown during midday hours, with stops along the way. Take a trolley ride to the Nautical History Center and the U.S.S. Kidd, the only ship to exhibit wartime camouflage paint. A ride on the trolley is free.

Baton Rouge is proud to be the home of Louisiana State University (LSU) and its many attributes and museums, among them the LSU Museum of Art and the LSU Rural Life Museum. In celebration of its agrarian/agricultural past, the Rural Life Museum has exhibit areas from prehistoric times to the early 20th century, including a working plantation and all the out-buildings necessary for a self-sustaining farm. The outdoor folk museum is divided into three sections: The Barn Area, The Plantation Area,

Louisiana Art & Science Museum.
Photo courtesy of
Louisiana Art & Science Museum.

and the Folk Architecture Area. Each area has several buildings recreated to the appropriate time period. A colorful asset is the 25-acre Windrush Gardens.

Here's exciting news for patrons of the arts. A project to create a downtown Baton Rouge arts district, a block from the Mississippi River and adjacent to the Old State Capitol, is set to open in late 2005. It's the Shaw Center for the Arts, soon to be a $5 million, 52,000 square foot museum of art, a performing arts center and arts workshop facilities. The project is a joint venture of LSU, the City of Baton Rouge, and the State of Louisiana. Additionally, the Shaw Center will house the LSU Museum of Art, which is now housed in LSU's Memorial Tower. Included at the center will be a venue for theater performances, rehearsal space, classrooms, and arts education projects.

The Louisiana Office of Tourism told us that they've launched a Wetland Birding Trail, a nature-based trail comprised of more than 100 sites and loops for 22 parishes. Birds and other wildlife make this a popular outing and Louisiana's link to the Great Gulf Coast Birding Trail that extends from the Yucatan Peninsula to Southern Florida.

The Baton Rouge area is also known as Plantation Country because of the magnificent pre-Civil War plantations along the River Road. You've seen them in movies and magazines, and many are open for tours. Among them are the famous Oak Alley, the huge and

LOUISIANA'S HOMES OF HISTORY

Shadows-on-the-Teche in New Iberia is not only a marvelous old mansion, but it is one so important to the history of the region that it is a property of the National Trust for Historic Preservation. The house, begun around 1830 by master craftsman James Bedell for sugarcane planter David Weeks, is more modest than the huge and opulent homes built by some planters, but it is equally as grand in design and appointments. The architecture of the house fits perfectly with its location on the bayou.

The style of the coral-colored brick "Shadows" is Greek Revival, but adaptations were made to account for the climate, culture, and availability of materials, thus it features French Creole and Anglo-American influences. The house is a two and a half story, full masonry structure with three dormers across the front and rear. Eight Doric columns of stuccoed brick support a large entablature that extends the length of the front. Typical of colonial Louisiana homes, the interior design shows three rooms across and two rooms deep, both upstairs and down.

Clay from the banks of the Bayou Teche, just behind the house, was used to make the bricks, while the cypress trees from the swamp provided the wood for framing and flooring. The wife of the builder, Mary Clara Conrad Weeks, planted the massive, moss-draped live oak trees that provide shade for The Shadows. Unfortunately, David Weeks never lived in the house. When his wife and six children moved into the home in June 1834, Mr. Williams was at Yale Medical School in Connecticut trying to have his debilitating illness diagnosed. David Weeks died at Yale in August, 1834, never having seen his completed home.

After remaining in seclusion at The Shadows for years, Mary Weeks married Judge John Moore in 1841. That same year, Judge Moore was elected to Congress. They lived happily at The Shadows —entertaining lavishly and often —until the Civil War and the Yankee invasion of their home. When the Union officers came, the remaining family moved to the third floor, where Mary Weeks Moore died.

After great grandson Weeks Hall returned to The Shadows in the 1920s, among the visitors to the grand old home were Edmund Wilson, H.L. Mencken, Stark Young, Henry Miller, Max Ernst, Abe Rattner, Cecil B. deMille, May West, and Walt Disney.

A most amazing thing about The Shadows is that it remained in the same family for four generations, from the time it was built until heir Weeks Hall bequeathed his family home to the National Trust at his death in 1958.

Shadows-on-the-Teche is open daily except for Thanksgiving, Christmas, and New Years Day.

Houmas House is one of the state's most historic showplaces. It sits on land that was purchased from the Houmas Indians by a French planter who made his fortune in sugar cane. The early structure was in the style of a French country house; it was purchased in 1812 by South Carolinian Wade Hampton, a decorated general in the Revolutionary War. Later, Hampton's son-in-law bought the home and remodeled it in a Greek Revival style.

After growing about 20,000 acres of sugar cane for 20 years, Houmas House owners sold it to Irishman John Burnside. When Union officers tried to take the house during the Civil War, Burnside refused to relinquish it. He said that as a British subject he was exempt from the take-over.

Houmas House was one Louisiana's largest sugar cane plantations; it produced 20 million pounds of sugar yearly. This grand home, recently reopened to public tours, features fine period antiques and a collection of Old Paris Porcelain. Latil's Landing restaurant now occupies the old French House, c.1770. Houmas House is about 30 miles south of Baton Rouge.

Other favorite antebellum homes include **Madewood,** a fabulous Greek Revival mansion in Napoleanville. This home, located on the Bayou Lafourche, was designed by architect Henry Howard, who also designed the opulent Nottoway. It is a National Historic Landmark and also available for overnight guests. Stay here, and see what Southern splendor is all about! This one is featured in prestigious national magazines. It's about 45 miles from Baton Rouge.

Destrehan (c. 1787) is the oldest documented plantation house extant in the Mississippi Valley. Magnificent oaks make this one even more outstanding. It has a museum store and antiques, and is only eight miles from the New Orleans International Airport.

The elegant **San Francisco** on the old East Bank of the River Road near Garyville, about 25 minutes from New Orleans, was built c. 1850 by Edmond Marmillion. Rumor has it that this was the setting for the novel, *Steamboat Gothic,* by Frances Parkinson Keyes. The style has been called "steamboat Gothic" because it resembles decorative elements on old riverboats. It started out as Sans Frusquin, though mispronunciations gave it the name San Francisco.

Nottoway on the Great River Road near White Castle is like an ornate wedding cake rising from the soil. Built around 1857-59, it is the South's largest plantation, boasting 64 rooms, including a huge ballroom. Native Virginian John Hampden Randolph wanted a showplace and hired noted architect Henry Howard to design it. Randolph named his grand home for a county in Virginia.

Nottoway Plantation on the River Road.
Photo courtesy of Louisiana Office of Tourism.

Vacherie is the place where several plantations are located, perhaps none more beautiful than the enchanting **Oak Alley** (c. 1839), a National Historic Landmark. The home peeks shyly through an oak alley, where 28 massive trees line up as if to protect the home. A gift shop, an ice cream parlor, and overnight lodging in cabins are available.

Evergreen (c. 1832) is an intact plantation complex, with 37 buildings to its credit, all on the National Register. The grand Greek Revival house can now be toured, as well as many of the out buildings. There are 22 slave cabins on site, and now, there's a tour of a Mississippi River swamp and oxbow lake, available by swamp buggy! The Victorian House on the property serves as a restaurant. It's near Vacherie, and so is **St. Joseph's Plantation**, where 19th century architect Henry Hobson Richardson was born. This house features Creole architecture; it has cottages, too. Another Creole plantation in the Vacherie area is the lovely **Laura** (c. 1805). This one has an unusual twist: tours based on Laura's memoirs. Hear about the life of Creole women and children in this memorable tour.

And then there's the town of **St. Francisville**, where more gracious homes are waiting to be toured. The town itself is worth a tour. Don't miss nearby **Rosedown**, now a State Historic Site. The home was built around 1835 by Daniel Turnbull for his bride, a Miss Barrow of Greenwood Plantation. Greenwood was built c. 1830 as a typical Greek Revival. It has been restored after a fire in 1960 and was the setting for the television series "North and South."

Oakley was built in 1810 as the result of a Spanish Land grant obtained in 1770. The owners had a daughter who needed help with her social skills. They found and hired a young man to stay with them to tutor the daughter and teach her drawing and the finer pursuits. The young man was John James Audubon. See it now as the Audubon State Historic Site. Audubon painted 32 of his famous birds here. **Butler Greenwood** Plantation is near St. Francisville, still resplendent since 1790s. **The Myrtles** in St. Francisville is said to be haunted, and perhaps it's the power of suggestion, but when I visited the place, I felt a presence.

These are a few of the many fine old homes along the Louisiana side of the Mississippi River. We wish we had enough space to include each one, for they are all historically significant and outstanding. If we missed your favorite, please forgive. As of this writing, they are open for daily tours; some offer B&B lodging and restaurants, and all have admission fees.

opulent Nottoway, Destrehan, Evergreen, Houmas House, Madewood, Greenwood, Rosedown, The Myrtles, and more. The Old South lives here in the architecture, antiques, and moss-laden oaks. Find them around Baton Rouge in the towns of **Vacherie, White Castle, Napoleanville**, and the picture-perfect **St. Francisville**.

Many of the antebellum homes are in and around St. Francisville, sometimes referred to as "English Louisiana" because of the English settlers who came when the area was part of England's West Florida. Today, the town is a treasure-trove of historic architecture, including the serene and lovely Grace Episcopal Church; the church parish was organized in 1828.

Oak Alley Plantation on the River Road.
Photo courtesy of Louisiana Office of Tourism.

New Orleans

Next stop — New Orleans. Expect the unexpected in sites, street scenes and sumptuous food. New Orleans is often called "the city that care forgot," and I might add the city where it is essential to forget one four letter word: diet. Enter the most European of all the American cities, one known for its colorful history, jazz music, and sensational food. One of the most wonderful things about this gourmand's delight is that many of the fine restaurants are family owned and operated, which means that the menus and preparation are unique and tasty rather than institutional and bland.

The best known parts of town are Uptown, the lovely Garden District, the Riverfront, and the inimitable French Quarter, also called Vieux Carré or simply "the

Artists in Jackson Square, New Orleans.

Quarter" by those who know and love it. The Quarter encompasses about 90 blocks between Canal Street, Rampart Street, Esplanade Avenue and the Mississippi River. The best time and place to start a tour here is early morning, when things are quiet and beignets and café au lait are waiting at Café Du Monde near Jackson Square. Afterward, find a shop that sells pralines – a special New Orleans treat — and stock up.

MARDI GRAS!

Mardi Gras has single-handedly enhanced New Orleans' reputation as "the city that care forgot" for during this festive event, all cares are forgotten. With all the noise and hard-core reveling that takes place during Mardi Gras, it's hard to remember that this time of high frivolity is a holy Catholic celebration. Here's the story...

It seems that the fluctuating date of Mardi Gras was established by the Catholic Church when the church designed the Gregorian calendar. They planned fixed days for Christmas, but chose moveable days for other religious holidays. Mardi Gras takes place 46 days preceding Easter, accounting for the 40 days of Lent plus six Sundays. Carnival season officially opens on the Epiphany twelve days after Christmas and ends the day before Ash Wednesday. We know this day as Fat Tuesday, the last chance to eat, drink, and be merry before the Lenten season of fasting and repentance.

The Church may not condone the racy revelry but lacks control over people's actions once they've consumed large quantities of liquid spirits. The Church does, however, insist on a strict period of prayer and fasting afterward.

The French began their organized celebration of Mardi Gras shortly after New Orleans was founded in 1718, though Mobile, Alabama, claims to be the first Mardi Gras city. Later, when the Spanish governors arrived, they banned the observance and the ban continued until 1823, when the Catholic Creoles in the French Quarter got permission to hold masquerade balls. Three years later they began wearing masks on the street and parades followed suit. The New Orleans paper at the time, the *Daily Picayune,* published the first account of a Mardi Gras in 1837.

Over the years, the parades became more colorful and festive and secret societies, or krewes, were organized. The first was the Mistick Krewe of Comus, originally founded to return civility to the wild shenanigans of Mardi Gras. The Comus krewe also started the practice of elaborate, private balls with their own designated King and Queen reigning over the event.

It was the Krewe of Rex that began the tradition of throwing things from floats. Trinkets became "doubloons" and today's colorful beaded necklaces are popular souvenirs. "Throw me something, Mister!" is a resounding yell along the parade route and literally thousands of people scramble to catch the prizes.

Mardi Gras in New Orleans is unlike any other event in this country.

People fill the streets of the French Quarter to capacity on parade days; they hang out windows and lean over balconies. The order of the day is uncontrolled chaos, and the young and adventurous love it!

Learn more about Mardi Gras in New Orleans at Blaine Kern's Mardi Gras World on the west bank of the Mississippi River in Algiers Point. Take a free ferry across the river to see the creation of Mardi Gras costumes, the building of a fleet of floats, and other pertinent items used exclusively for the celebration. There's a gift shop, too.

And then there's the Cajun Mardi Gras! Lafayette has one, not as wild and chaotic as New Orleans, but still quite festive, with parades and royalty. King Gabriel and Queen Evangeline hold court at this event. Balls and colorful parties are held here, too.

Acadiana's Courrie de Mardi Gras, the rural one, is completely unique in the world. Masked horsemen adorned in capes ride through the bayou-land asking farm families, in French, if they will "receive the Mardi Gras." The bands of masked riders have a captain, who actually approaches the farm waving a white flag. When the people grant permission, the other horsemen ride in, dismount, and commence to dance and sing before gathering the ingredients for a huge community gumbo. Among the donated ingredients are live chickens, rice, onions, flour, and filé.

The "Riding of the Mardi Gras" usually concludes with a big fais-do-do and pots of gumbo for riders and families. This is a much anticipated event in Cajun country in such places as Church Point and Mamou.

"Courrie de Mardi Gras" or Riding the Mardi Gras in Cajunland's Church Point. Photo courtesy of Louisiana Office of Tourism.

Look closely at the architecture in the Quarter, especially the lacy iron balconies and court yard gates, and spend time in Jackson Square, where artists are usually set up by mid-morning near the spectacular St. Louis Cathedral. Also around Jackson Square, street musicians often perform for gratuities. Jazz aficionados will find Preservation Hall, where known musicians jam nightly, usually to a packed house. If you're lucky, perhaps you'll hear a member of the Marsalis family.

Building in New Orleans' French Quarter.

St. Louis Cathedral, New Orleans.
Photo courtesy of Louisiana Office of Tourism.

Unless you adore noise and chaos, you may want to leave the city to Mardi Gras revelers in February. The Quarter is packed and hotels and restaurants are full during Mardi Gras week. Mardi Gras is a time when anything goes and usually does. That's one reason the city is also called "The Big Easy."

Whether you call it NOLA, the City that Care Forgot, the Big Easy, the City of Jazz, the Crescent City, or the South's Sin City, expect to find magic in this old town. Here you can still ride a streetcar, visit an authentic oyster bar, have a Bananas Foster exquisite dessert, stay overnight in a quaint Bed & Breakfast inn or small intimate hotel in the Quarter, visit the popular Audubon Park Zoo, or shop for amazing antiques along the seven blocks of Royal Street between Iberville and Dumaine.

The New Orleans Museum of Art is one of the finest in the South. The museum began in 1910, thanks to sugar broker Isaac Delgado, who funded it. The Greek Revival-style building is home to 46 galleries, including outstanding permanent collections and international traveling exhibits. French artists include the Impressionists Claude Monet and Edgar Degas, also Raoul Dufy, Joan Miró, and Pablo Picasso. Don't miss the decorative arts and the Fabergé Gallery. This museum does the city proud. There are people who go to great lengths to collect Newcomb Pottery. See why at the Newcomb Art Gallery at Tulane's Woldenberg Art Center near Audubon Park. This is a must for pottery lovers. Visit Audubon Park's 58 acres and 1500 animals that live here, many are rare and endangered species. The Swamp Exhibit is excellent!

The Faubourg Marigny (say Mar-i-nee) area is a current hot spot, with good restaurants, shopping, and B&B inns. Popular nightclubs are found on Frenchmen Street, and it's very close to the French Quarter. In the Quarter, Magazine Street offers diverse shops, many of which are in high-ceilinged, 19th century cottages situated among residences and restaurants. The shops are colorful, interesting, and eclectic, and much time can be spent here. Expect fine antiques and art galleries in this area. Longue Vue House and Gardens is an eight-acre city estate that offers an interesting foray into the lifestyles of the super rich. The Classic Revival-style mansion contains rare English antiques and fine decorative arts, as collected by owners Edgar and Edith Stern. He was a cotton broker *cum* philanthropist; she was a Sears heiress. The estate is open daily except for major holidays.

After the bustling city of New Orleans, you may be ready for the relative quiet of the clean and green Magnolia State, Mississippi...but first, find a few Louisiana recipes sure to tempt the taste buds of those who like a little spice in life.

ROLLING THE DICE IN DIXIE

There was a time when big spending Southerners got together and chartered a plane to Las Vegas for a week or so of gambling. Some returned jubilant at the amount of their winnings while others were heartsick at having lost so much of their hard-earned money. Those Vegas jaunts are long gone except for special occasions because casinos are now readily available in our own Deep South.

Luckily for non-smokers except for casinos on the property of Native Americans, the land-locked "boats" are on or near water of some sort. It's a good bet that non-smokers — now about 80 percent of Americans — appreciate access to fresh air and cool breezes to keep from being barbecued by storm-strength clouds of cigarettes and cigar smoke. Perhaps smokers are drawn to gambling, or is it that the adrenalin rush of a winning streak – or the anguish of losing – lay the foundation for a tobacco fix.

Whatever the reason for the rush, there are ample choices for those who wish to partake of Las Vegas at a Southern site. If your game of chance choice is slots, blackjack, roulette, craps, keno, poker, or baccarat, you'll find it in abundance in Mississippi and Louisiana, though there are few (three) casinos to date in Alabama, fans find their way to the nearby Mississippi Gulf Coast casinos, the Choctaw establishments near Philadelphia, MS, the plethora of casinos in Mississippi along the Mississippi River, and New Orleans.

As of this writing, the three American Indian-owned casinos are the Creek Entertainment Center in Atmore, the Riverside Entertainment Center in Wetumpka, and the Tallapoosa Entertainment Center in Montgomery. A $300 million complex is scheduled to open at Wetumpka in a few years.

The Mississippi Gulf Coast towns of Biloxi, Gulfport, and Bay St. Louis now have a dozen or so casinos, with the big Beau Rivage Hotel and Casino a favorite plush property. Casino gaming and entertainment are the Mississippi Beach's newest attraction, with golf, sun, sand, and Gulf waters an added benefit.

Elsewhere in Mississippi, find nine casinos in Tunica, southeast of Memphis; one in Lula and two in Greenville. Further down the Mississippi River, Vicksburg is home to four casinos, with Natchez hosting one. Choctaw, near Philadelphia, now offers two, including a resort casino with a championship golf course.

For more information on Mississippi's casinos, contact the Mississippi Gaming Commission at 1/866.948.1144; www.mississippi-gaming.org, or 1/866.SEE MISS.

Louisiana's riverboat casinos are thriving, too, with Shreveport/Bossier City reminding us of little Nevada. The cities, separated by the Red River, were once bastions of the Bible Belt. Perhaps they still are, but the glitzy and glamorous casino hotels are the most visible from Interstate-20. One high-rise hotel looks like a tall copper structure standing guard over the cities. With Shreveport's two and Bossier's four casinos – and the big Louisiana Downs thoroughbred horse racing track – the northwest corner of the state is surely a gaming destination for the Ark-La-Tex. Since Shreveport is only three hours from Dallas, Texans come, too.

Downstate, Lake Charles's new $365 million L'Auberge du Lac

resort is a hot new property of Las Vegas-based Pinnacle Entertainment. It's one of two casinos in Lake Charles and big things are expected since it's so close to the gaming enthusiasts in and around Houston, Texas.

Louisiana's land-based American Indian casinos are located in Charenton, Kinder, and Marksville. The largest casino concentration is in New Orleans, with four casinos are permanently docked on the Mississippi River. Of course, gaming is just one of the many attractions in this major U.S. destination.

For more information on gaming in Louisiana, contact the Office of Tourism at 225.342.8119; www.LouisianaTravel.com.

Float in Mardi Gras' Rex Parade, New Orleans.
Photo courtesy of Louisiana Office of Tourism.

THIS 'N THAT ...

- The nation's first opera was performed in New Orleans in 1796.

- The name "Jazz" was first given to the music of New Orleans about 100 years ago. New Orleanian Louis "Satchmo" Armstrong helped make jazz popular world-wide.

- Elvis Prestley got his start at The Louisiana Hayride in Shreveport.

LOUISIANA RECIPES

Louisiana is as famous for its cuisine as for its *joie de vivre*. New Orleans is full of world-class restaurants, perhaps more per capita than any other place in the country. Some restaurants have been in the same family for generations, and the food is made from scratch, which is what makes the food here so special. In a nation of micro-waved and institutionalized food, it is indeed a pleasure to find a place where the culinary arts are still practiced.

You may find either "Creole" or "Cajun" somewhere on Louisiana menus, so we'll try to explain the difference for visitors to the state. Cajun is more down-home, country cooking perfected by great grandmother and passed down, usually seasoned with spices and herbs. The base of Cajun food is the "roux," certainly the foundation of sauces and gravies, Creole food is tomato based.

"First you make a roux..." is the beginning of every good Cajun recipe. It's the foundation that builds delicious, spicy food and it's a mixture of fat and flour that's best if made in a black iron skillet; a well-seasoned one, of course. The two ingredients are cooked together over medium heat, stirring constantly, until dark brown but not burned. A good goal is to let it reach the color of coffee with a touch of cream. The key is constant, moderate heat and constant stirring.

ROUX

4 tabsp. lard or cooking oil   4 tabsp. flour

Melt lard or oil; add flour and stir until the roux becomes a very dark, rich, reddish brown. Do not let the mixture burn! *Some chefs add a chopped onion and 1/2 bell pepper to keep roux from burning.* The roux serves as a thickening agent, but it also imparts a distinct flavor from the browning of the flour. Double the recipe for larger quantities. Culinary success starts with a perfect roux.

HOT CRAB APPETIZERS

1 (6 oz.) can crab meat, drained	2 tabsp. butter
2 tabsp. sherry	2 tabsp. flour
1 teasp. salt	1 egg yolk
Dash of white pepper	1 cup light cream
1 tabsp. marjoram	6 slices white bread

Combine first five ingredients, then set aside. In saucepan, melt butter, remove from heat and stir in flour. Beat egg yolk into cream. Stir cream into the butter-flour mixture and heat until thickened, stirring constantly. Mixture will be very thick. Pour sauce on crab mixture and toss. Using a small cookie cutter, cut four rounds from each slice of bread. Toast rounds on one side only. Mound crab meat on untoasted side of each round. Place under broiler until lightly browned. Serve hot; makes 24 appeteizers.

ARTICHOKE BITS

1 (14 oz.) can artichoke hearts, drained	1/2 cup olive oil
2 lemons	1 cup seasoned bread crumbs

Quarter the artichoke hearts and squeeze the lemon juice over them. Dip hearts in the olive oil and roll them in the bread crumbs. Place on a greased cookie sheet and bake at 400 degrees F. for ten to fifteen minutes. Makes 32.

SHRIMP DIP

4 oz. cream cheese	1 can shrimp
2 teasp. lemon juice	1 (8 oz.) sour cream
1 pkg. Italian dressing mix	

Drain shrimp and cut into small pieces. Mix the cream cheese, lemon juice, dressing mix, shrimp and sour cream well. Excellent when served with chips or party crackers.

CRAWFISH RICH AND ELEGANT

1 lb. crawfish tails	3 tabsp. flour
1/2 cup butter	1 pint Half & Half
1 bunch green onions, chopped	3 tabsp. sherry
1/2 cup chopped parsley	Salt and red pepper to taste

In a skillet sauté the crawfish in one-fourth cup of the butter for ten minutes. Remove to a bowl. Saute' the green onion and parsley in the remaining butter and blend in the flour. Gradually add the cream, stirring constantly, to make a thick sauce. Add the sherry, crawfish, salt and red pepper. This may be used as a party dip or an entrée!

JEZEBEL SAUCE

1 (16 oz.) jar pineapple preserves	2 tabsp. Dijon mustard
1 (16 oz.) jar apple jelly	1 (5 oz.) jar horseradish
1(2 oz.) tin dry mustard	

Let a block of cream cheese soften. Mix all five ingredients above to make sauce. Pour a small amount of sauce over block of cream cheese. Serve with party crackers. Sauce keeps in refrigerator for weeks. Makes about 4-1/2 cups.

BAYOU TECHE PARTY CHEESE

2 lbs. Brie or Camembert cheese, unpeeled	1-1/2 stick butter
	1 (4 oz.) pkg. almonds

Clarify butter. Add almonds to butter; heat over medium heat until almonds become gold in color. Pour this mixture over cheese. Heat in microwave until cheese begins to puff (about 1 to 1-1/2 minutes), but crust does not break. Serve with party crackers.

OLIVE CURRY

2 (5 oz.) jars olives, drained and chopped	1/2 teasp. salt
1 cup chopped green onions	1/2 teasp. curry powder
1 cup mayonnaise	Red pepper to taste, optional
3 cups sharp cheese, grated	3 or 4 English muffins

Mix all ingredients and place on cut side of toasted, buttered English muffin. Broil until cheese melts and browns slightly. Cut muffins into fourths and serve hot.

SPINACH SALAD

4 or 5 strips bacon, fried crisp
  and crumbled
2 tabsp. bacon drippings
1/3 cup virgin olive oil
1 tabsp. Dijon mustard
3 tabsp. Worcestershire
2 tabsp. brown sugar
1/3 cup red wine
Wash and drain 5 large
  handsful spinach, torn into
  bite-sized pieces
Seasoned salt

Fry bacon. Remove; place on paper towel to drain. Add olive oil and remaining ingredients (except spinach) to bacon drippings. Heat and pour sauce over spinach to wilt. Add crumbled bacon and garnish with cherry tomatoes. Serves 3 – 4.

GERMAN SALAD

1 (16 oz.) can sauerkraut
2 cups sugar
2/3 cup vinegar
1/4 cup chopped onion
2 cups chopped celery
1/2 cup green pepper,
  chopped

Drain sauerkraut; rinse and drain again. Bring sugar and vinegar to a boil. Cool. Mix sauerkraut, celery, onions and green pepper and pour syrup over all. Refrigerate 24 hours before serving. Serves about 10. *Will keep nicely in refrigerator for days.*

SUMMER SALAD SUPREME

1 (8 oz.) pkg. cream cheese
3/4 cup sugar
1 (15-1/4 oz.) can crushed
  pineapple, drained
1 (10 oz.) pkg. frozen
  strawberries
1/2 cup chopped nuts
1 (8 oz.) carton Cool Whip

Soften cream cheese; blend with sugar. Mix pineapple, strawberries and nuts. Add Cool Whip. Combine with cheese mixture. Place in lightly oiled 9 x 13 pan or Pyrex. Freeze several hours or overnight. Serves about 15.

ACADIAN ARTICHOKE CASSEROLE

2 (14 oz.) cans artichoke
  hearts, reserve liquid
1 (1 lb. 8 oz.) box Italian
  bread crumbs
1/2 cup virgin olive oil
Juice of 2 lemons
2 cloves garlic, minced
1 cup Romano cheese,
  grated
Salt and pepper to taste

Mix artichoke juice, crumbs, olive oil, and lemon juice Mash artichokes thoroughly and add to above mixture, add cheese and garlic. Blend well. Place in a 2-1/2 quart casserole and bake in a 350° oven for about 20 minutes. Serves 6 – 8.

PEAS EPICUREAN

1 can petit pois peas	1 tabsp. flour
1 cup heavy ceam	Salt and pepper to taste
4 strips bacon	Dash Worcestershire sauce
1/2 large onion, chopped	and Accent, if desired
1 cup mushrooms, sliced	1/4 cup sherry

Chop bacon and sauté with onion until brown; add mushrooms and sauté. Add flour and cream, stirring constantly over low heat. After sauce has thickened and is smooth, add seasonings and sherry. Add peas last, gently folding into mixture. Serves 4.

BROCCOLI CASSEROLE

2 (10 oz.) pkgs. frozen, chopped broccoli	2 eggs, slightly beaten
1 cup mayonnaise	2 large onions, chopped
1 cup shredded Cheddar cheese	

Cook broccoli for five minutes. Drain. Mix together mayonnaise, cheese, eggs and onions. Fold broccoli into mixture. Top with buttered bread crumbs. Bake in 350° oven for 45 minutes. Serves 6.

CAJUN RED BEANS 'N RICE

1 lb. red kidney beans (soak overnight in enough water to cover)	1 bell pepper, diced
	2 bay leaves
	2 sprigs thyme
4 tabsp. bacon drippings	Salt and red pepper to taste
1 large onion, minced	Tabasco to taste
1 ham hock or ham slice	4 cups water

After soaking, rinse and drain beans well. Melt fat in large pot and sauté onion. Add beans and remaining ingredients. Cover and cook over low heat about four hours, stirring occasionally. A pinch of sugar may be added if desired. Serve over hot cooked rice; add smoked sausage, if desired. Serves about 8.

INDIAN CORN

6 tabsp. oil	2 cups milk
1 large onion, chopped	1 cup corn meal
1 cup creamed corn	1 egg, beaten
Salt and red pepper to taste	1/4 cup green onion tops

Saute' onion in oil until transparent. Add corn and season with salt and red pepper. Add milk and slowly stir in corn meal. Remove from heat when thickened and stir in beaten egg. Bake in buttered casserole at 350° until brown, 35-40 minutes. Serves 6.

SWEET POTATO/BOURBON CASSEROLE

3 (17 oz) cans sweet potatoes	1/3 cup bourbon whiskey
1/2 cup brown sugar	1/2 stick butter
One large orange rind, grated	1 teasp. salt
1/2 cup orange juice	

Layer sweet potatoes in a buttered casserole. Sprinkle with brown sugar, add orange juice, orange rind, and bourbon. Dot with butter, cover and bake at 350° for about 45 minutes, or until all the juice has been absorbed. Serves 6-8.

BAKED CHEESE GARLIC GRITS

1 cup grits	2 eggs, well beaten
4 cups water	1/4 cup milk
1 teasp. salt	Salt, pepper and red pepper
1 roll garlic cheese	to taste
1 stick butter	

Cook grits in water with salt according to package directions. Cut in chunks and add roll of garlic cheese and butter. When cheese and butter have melted, add eggs, milk, salt and peppers. Grease (with butter) 1-1/2 quart casserole and bake about 45 – 60 minutes in 350° oven. Serves 6 – 8. *If you prefer, use roll of Jalapeno cheese instead of garlic cheese.*

VEGETARIAN PASTA PRIMAVERA

1 cup broccoli pieces	2 cups chopped tomatoes
1/2 cup fresh mushrooms, sliced	1/2 cup Parmesan cheese, grated
2 tabsp. butter	1/4 teasp. oregano leaves
7 or 8 oz. pkg fettucini, cooked and drained	1/4 teasp. basil leaves

Saute' broccoli and mushrooms in butter. Toss with fettucini and remaining ingredients; heat thoroughly. Sprinkle with additional cheese, if desired. Serves 6.

JAMBALAYA
(Old South Louisiana Recipe!)

1 lb. shrimp, cleaned
2 tabsp. lard (or oil)
1 medium onion, minced
1/2 bell pepper, finely
   chopped
2 cloves garlic, minced

3 cups chopped smoked ham
1 (8 oz.) can tomato sauce
1-1/2 cups uncooked rice
Salt and red pepper to taste

Cook shrimp, reserving 2 cups of liquid. Place minced onion, bell pepper and garlic in hot lard. Add shrimp and chopped ham; sauté about five minutes. Add tomato sauce and rice with shrimp liquid. Season to taste. Boil lightly until rice is well done. Add small amount of water if necessary. Serves 6 to 8.

BEST BRISKET

10 lb. brisket
Salt, red and black pepper
   to taste
Accent
Garlic salt
Dry mustard

1-1/2 cups vegetable oil
1/2 cup lemon juice (fresh)
1 cup red wine, dry
2 tabsp. Worcestershire sauce
2 tabsp. dried parsley

Season brisket with salt, red and black pepper, Accent and garlic salt. Best if seasoned heavily. Coat with dry mustard. Place in marinade of oil, lemon juice, wine, parsley and Worcestershire sauce. Bake in marinade at 225° oven for about 8 hours; more if brisket is larger. Serves about 16.

CHICKEN BREAST CLOUTIERVILLE

6 chicken breast halves,
   deboned
6 slices bacon
1 jar dried beef
1 can cream of chicken soup

1 cup sour cream
1 tabsp. grated onion
1 (3 oz.) pkg. cream cheese
1 pkg. slivered almonds

Wrap unsalted chicken in bacon. Place layer of dried beef in baking pan; place wrapped chicken breast on top of beef. Mix soup with next three ingredients; pour over chicken. Cover pan lightly with foil. Bake two hours in 325° oven. Remove foil and let brown. Toast almonds and sprinkle over top just before serving. Serve over rice. Serves 6.

CRAWFISH ÉTOUFFÉE

2 level teasp. flour	1 lbs. peeled crawfish tails
1 stick butter or oleo	and extra portion of fat
1 medium onion, chopped	1/4 cup parsley, minced
2 tabsp. green pepper,	1/4 teasp red pepper
chopped fine	2 green onions, minced
1 stalk celery	1/2 teasp salt
1 dash garlic (optional)	

Melt butter and stir in flour. Add onion, garlic, green pepper, anc celery. Cook about 30 minutes. Add fat and cook 20 minutes. Add tails and cook 20 minutes. Add other ingredients and simmer about 20 – 30 minutes. Serve over rice. With French Bread and a green salad this recipe serves 6.

SEAFOOD OKRA GUMBO

1 quart okra, cut into	1/4 cup parsley, chopped
1/2 inch pieces	1 (16 oz.) can stewed tomatoes
2 tabsp. cooking oil	2 bay leaves
Water	2 tabsp. Worcestershire sauce
2 to 3 lbs. shrimp	2 small boiled crabs
2/3 cup oil	Salt to taste
1/2 cup flour	1/2 teasp. black pepper
2 medium onions, chopped	1/2 teasp. red pepper
1 bell pepper, chopped	
2 ribs celery, chopped	
2 cloves garlic, chopped	

Wash, peel and devien shrimp. Set shrimp aside in refrigerator; boil shrimp shells in two quarts water for several hours to make stock. Set aside. In heavy iron skillet, heat two tablespoons oil and sauté the okra until "ropiness" is gone, about one-half hour. Set aside. In a large black iron Dutch oven, make a dark brown roux with the oil and flour, stirring constantly to brown but do not burn. While cooking roux, add onions, bell pepper, celery, garlic and parsley and sauté until tender. Add tomatoes and cook 15 minutes. Add sautéed okra, shrimp stock, crabs (broken into quarters), bay leaves, Worchestershire sauce, black and red pepper. Bring to a slow boil and simmer for about two hours, stirring occasionally. Add salt to taste. Add the peeled shrimp and continue cooking until shrimp are done. Serve over steamed rice. This gumbo is better if cooked a day ahead and refrigerated overnight. Serves 8-10. *This recipe is attributed to the Gumbo Shop in New Orleans.*

BANANAS FOSTER

2 cups brown sugar
4 bananas
1/2 lb. butter

Vanilla ice cream
6 oz. white rum

Heat sugar and butter in chafing dish until sugar melts. Quarter bananas (cut lengthwise, then half); add banana pieces to butter and sugar. Cook three minutes, add rum and cook two minutes more. Serve over ice cream. Serves 8.

LOUISIANA PECAN PIE

3 eggs
3/4 cup sugar
1 cup cane syrup
1/8 teasp. salt
2 tabsp. melted butter

1 teasp. vanilla
1 cup pecans
1 (9 inch) unbaked pie shell

Beat eggs slightly. Add next five ingredients; mix well. Fold in pecans; pour into unbaked pastry shell and bake in 400° oven for 15 minutes. ; reduce temperature to 350°; bake about 40 minutes more, or until knife inserted near center comes out clean. Do not overbake. If crust browns too much, cover top lightly with foil.

FABULOUS FRUIT PIE

2 eggs, beaten
1 cup sugar
1 stick butter
1 teasp. vanilla

1/2 cup coconut
1/2 cup raisins
1/2 cup chopped pecans
1 (9-inch) pie shell

Mix first seven ingredients and place in pie shell. Heat oven to 400° before putting in pie, then turn oven to 300° and let pie bake 30 minutes.

APPLE PRALINE PIE

1/2 cup brown sugar	1/2 teasp. salt
1/2 teasp. cinnamon	1 can (1 lb.) sliced apples
1/2 teasp. nutmeg	Pastry for two-crust pie
1 tabsp. quick-cooking	2 tabsp. butter
tapioca	Praline Topping
	Chopped nuts

Mix sugar, spices, tapioca and salt together. Drain syrup from apples, adding water, if necessary, to make 1/4 cup, and mix with apples and tapioca mixture. Pour into an unbaked eight-inch pastry-lined pie pan. Dot with butter. Cover with top pastry, cutting slits to allow steam to escape. Bake in a hot oven, 425°, about 45 minutes, until almost done. Spread Praline Topping on top crust and sprinkle with 1/4 cup coarsely chopped nuts; continue to bake an additional five minutes.

PRALINE TOPPING: Cream two tablespoons butter until smooth; add 1/4 cup firmly packed brown sugar and one tablespoon light cream; beat until smooth.

NEW ORLEANS PRALINES

1-1/2 cups sugar	1/4 teasp. salt
3/4 cups light brown sugar	6 tabsp. butter
1/2 cup milk	1-1/2 cup chopped pecans
1 teasp. vanilla	

Combine the sugars, milk, vanilla, salt and butter in a heavy saucepan. Place over medium-high heat and bring to a boil, stirring once or twice. Boil for about six or seven minutes, or until the syrup reaches the soft-ball stage. Remove from heat and stir the mixture until it cools and thickens. When it is slightly thickened, add the pecans and spoon onto a large piece of waxed paper to cool and become firm. Store in plastic bags, or freeze until needed.

BREAD PUDDING

9 slices white bread	1 teasp. vanilla
1-1/4 cups sugar	4 egg yolks
1 (13 oz.) can evaporated	1/3 cup melted butter
milk	4 egg whites
2 cups fresh milk	

Break bread into small pieces. Place in mixing bowl with one cup sugar, evaporated milk, two cups milk, vanilla, egg yolks and melted butter. Mix well; pour into 10x8x2 baking pan. Bake in pre-heated oven 450° for 15 minutes. Remove and make meringue. Beat egg whites with 1/4 sugar until stiff. Cover pudding with meringue and rebake for 3 or 4 minutes until meringue is golden.

Serves 12. May be served with rum sauce, if desired. *This recipe is attributed to Don's Seafood Restaurants in Louisiana.*

RUM SAUCE

1 cup Carnation milk
1 cup fresh milk
1 cup sugar
1-1/2 tabsp. corn starch

3 tabsp. butter
2 oz. Rum
3 or 4 drops food coloring, yellow

In a double boiler, put milk, sugar, and butter. When hot, dissolve cornstarch in a little water and add to hot milk. Stir until thick. Remove from fire, then add Rum and food coloring. Serves 12.

CAJUN CAKE

2 cups flour
1-1/2 cups sugar
2 teasp. baking soda

2 small cans crushed pineapple, with juice
2 eggs
Icing (recipe below)

Mix all ingredients well; bake in a square pan for 30 minutes at 350°. Cook and ice cake. *This is an old family recipe, handed down through generations*

ICING

1/2 can evaporated milk
1/4 lb. butter
3/4 cup sugar

1 pkg. coconut
1/2 cup chopped pecans

Cook evaporated milk, butter and sugar until very thick. Add coconut and pecans.

NEW ORLEANS CHOCOLATE PIE

1 cup sugar
2-1/2 - 3 tabsp. cocoa
2-1/2 tabsp. flour
Pinch of salt
1/4 cup butter

2 egg yolks, beaten
2 cups milk
1-1/2 teasp. vanilla
1 (10") pie crust, baked
Meringue

In large saucepan, combine sugar, cocoa, flour and salt. Add next three ingredients; cook mixture over low heat until thick. Stir in vanilla; pour the filling into the pie crust, cover with meringue. Bake at 350 degrees F for 12 to 15 minutes. Cool before cutting. Serves 8 to 10.

LOUISIANA'S AUDUBON GOLF TRAIL

When we remember that Louisiana is the "sportsman's paradise," we think of fishing, duck hunting, deer hunting, water sports and more, but the state is also encouraging golfers to partake of the golfing largesse. The Audubon Golf Trail is a welcome addition to the existing natural beauty of Louisiana, for many of the courses are built on or near sites offering outstanding scenery. Named for the painter John James Audubon, who created his famous bird paintings while working as a tutor here in the 1800s, the courses offer an opportunity for others to see and hear birds similar to those Audubon found so compelling.

Among the ten Audubon Trail courses are Carter Plantation near Springfield, designed by golf pro David Toms. It's a 7050 yard, par 72 course. The Island course near Plaquemine was once part of a sugar plantation dating back to the 1800s. Sugar cane can still be seen in parts of the course. Gray Plantation Golf Course near Lake Charles recently ranked third "Best new course in America" by *Golf Digest*.

New Orleans is pleased to be the home of the Tournament Players Club of Louisiana. It has earned the ranking of # 4 in the "Upscale Public Golf Courses" in Golf Digest's annual listing of the best new facilities in the USA. The TPC of Louisiana, designed by Pete Dye, opened in April 2004 as the 24th among the Tournament Players Clubs.

Between New Orleans and Baton Rouge, Pelican Point in Gonzales, just off the banks of the Mississippi River, is also behind the historic Houmas House Plantation. Players say it's like a bit of Great Britain with a South Louisiana flavor. Ferris Land Design built the course on 250 acres that includes 30 acres of meandering lakes.

Golf resorts include The Bluffs on Thompson Creek north of Baton Rouge, where the 18-hole course was designed by Arnold Palmer, and Toro Hills, near Hodges Gardens and Toldeo Bend (between Many and Leesville). For more information on golf opportunities in Louisiana, see more at www.LouisianaTravel.com, or call 800.99.GUMBO.

MYSTERIOUS MARIE LAVEAU
The Voodoo Queen of New Orleans

Since Marie Laveau came on the scene as a voodoo practitioner, her name has evoked curiosity and trepidation among the believers. Even her place of birth is controversial. Some say she was born in New Orleans' French Quarter in 1794, while others say she was a native of the Caribbean islands. One rumor says that she was the daughter of a rich planter and a slave woman, and that she was part American Indian.

Whatever her origins, Marie Laveau managed to lend credence to voodooism in a town where Catholicism was dominant. In some instances, the mysterious Mariecombined the two, which in itself showed remarkable charisma. Perhaps it was her innate charisma that enabled her to convince her followers that she could make their wishes come true if they purchased one of her "charms," which may have been a rabbit's foot or the tail of a black cat. Whatever methods she used, Marie Laveau earned the reputation as a woman who made things happen. Straying husbands returned home; politicians won high office; lonely women found love and romance, much of which was attributed to Marie Laveau.

According to research, Marie Laveau was born a free mulatto in New Orleans. She married a carpenter, Jacques Paris, in 1819. Marie passed the word that Jacque was descended from a noble family in France, though it was said that he came from Santo Domingo. Marie and Jacque lived in the 1900 block of North Rampart Street. They lived quiet lives, though Marie attended a few voodoo meetings. Marie was beautiful, intelligent, but not educated, and a widow three years after her marriage to Jacques. She had to provide for herself, which she did initially by becoming a hairdresser to the ladies of New Orleans.

Hairdressing was the work that led to Marie's voodoo queen persona. While she worked on their hair, the ladies of the town began telling Marie of their problems with their husbands and their dreams for the future. Marie told them she could help by "putting a gris-gris (hex) on his doorstep." And so she did. She charged them for every gris gris and they paid dearly for her services. Marie was beautiful, stylish, and wise.

Voodooism was the current rage, and Marie Laveau capitalized on it. She wanted no part of the Devil worship that generally accompanied voodoo, so she devised her own form of voodooism that included favors for profit and the use of showmanship. She talked of a "monster serpent" from an Alabaster box, a black cat, a rooster, and other ritualistic methods that made her followers believe that she did indeed have power. The local media found her an interesting topic and enhanced her fame.

As her reputation grew, so did the sensual rituals held in the yard of her home, many of which were considered lewd. Marie dressed like a gypsy, with big gold earrings and bandanas, and she was often pregnant, a fact that did not stop her from dancing at the rituals, often with a snake wrapped around her body.

Marie Laveau, after enjoying a long life where a city full of people could not decide if she was good or evil, died in her sleep on June 16, 1881, at her cottage on St. Ann Street. She had lived there for half a century. During her last years, she renounced voodooism and embraced the Catholic faith. She is buried in St. Louis Cemetery No. 1, and still today, people visit her grave asking for wishes to be granted.

CAJUN WORDS AND PHRASES...

There's nothing that sounds better to me than an authentic Cajun accent, unless it's an Irish one. See below a few Cajun phrases.

- CHERE or CHER: It sounds like "share" and it means "dear" or some term of endearment. If a Cajun says "yes," the word does not evoke enthusiasm. If the response is "MAIS (say 'may') Yeah, Cher! " that's a very good sign.

- POOH-YI: Spoken as spelled. This Cajun expression denotes surprise or excitement or perhaps dismay. It's a popular exclamation that is sure to be heard in Cajun Country.

- ECRIVISSE: Pronounced as *ay-kree-veese*, it means that Cajun delicacy, crawfish!

- ANDOUILLE (ahn-<u>doo</u>-ee) and BOUDIN (<u>boo</u>-dan) are two types of spicy and delicious Cajun sausage.

- BEIGNET (bin-yay) is an oddly shaped doughnut without a hole. A favorite at Cafe du Monde in New Orleans.

- COMME CI, COMME CA (come-<u>see</u>, come-<u>sah</u>) is what Cajuns say when the response is "OK, I guess."

- BOUREE (<u>boo</u>-ray) is a card game often called Cajun bridge.

Au revoir, Cher!

MISSISSIPPI

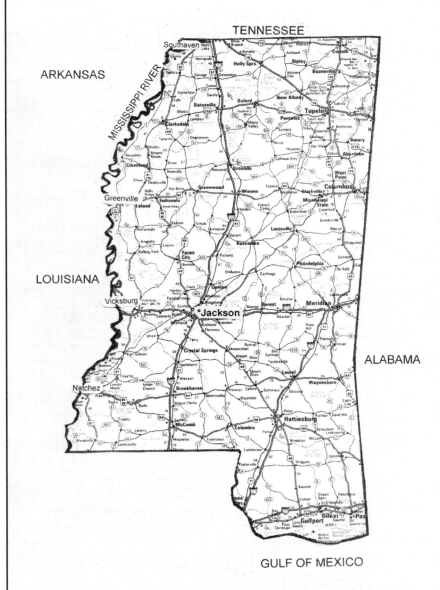

MISSISSIPPI FACTS

- Historic Jefferson College in Washington (just north of Natchez) was incorporated in 1802 as the first chartered educational institution in the Mississippi Territory.

- The voice of Darth Vader and "This is CNN News" is that of actor James Earl Jones, born in Tate County in 1931.

- The town of Grenada was formed when two rival towns, Pittsburgh and Tullahoma, were united in a symbolic wedding ceremony in 1836.

- Ole Miss is known for a lot of things, from its "Harvard of the South" reputation to the home of The Grove, where tailgatin' extraordinaire takes place, but it's also known as the place that houses an ancient Biblical manuscript, said to the oldest book in the United States.

- The first State Bar Association in the United States (for lawyers) was organized in Natchez in 1821.

- The nation's oldest land grant college for African Americans is Alcorn State University near Port Gibson.

- Jackson was once called "Chimneyville" because Union General William T. Sherman torched it in 1863. Not much was left standing but a few brick chimneys, thus the name.

- MTV (Music Television Video) was founded in 1981 by native Mississippian Bob Pittman when he was 32. Pittman hails from Brookhaven. His brother Tom is well-known in newspaper circles in the state.

- The Norris Bookbinding Company in Greenwood is the largest Bible re-binding plant in the nation.

- The Natchez Trace is thought to date back 8,000 years, for it was a trail made by buffaloes and native American Indians.

- The world's first human lung transplant was performed at University Medical Center in Jackson in 1963.

- The world's most widely used physiology textbook for physicians was published by Dr. Authur C. Guyton, a native of Oxford.

- The largest US Department of Agriculture (USDA) research facility is in the Delta town of Stoneville. Called the "Silicon Valley of Agriculture," agricultural researchers from Mississippi State University operate out of Stoneville.

MISSISSIPPI

INTRODUCTION

It seems that there's a new-found pride among Mississippians, and it is welcomed with open arms. This great state has gotten its share of less than flattering national press because of the past transgressions of so few people, but we believe that is changing. Thankfully, those who know the Magnolia State and her people pay little attention to outdated stereotypes of people who massacre the Queen's English in grammar, not Southern dialect. We wonder why news commentators seldom interview the many articulate and intelligent Mississippians who can and do create a positive impression. And why not occasionally mention the Nobel and Pulitzer Prize winners, the award-winning professionals from all fields, and the kind, generous people who live their daily lives volunteering in their communities and trying to help make the world a better place. We'd like to hear more about these good, decent people who love home and country, honor tradition, and place great emphasis on the old-fashioned word that still means so much. That word is "character."

Mississippians are proud of the entertainers, musicians, artists, writers and sports heroes who hail from this Deep South state, probably more per capita than any other state in the union. Among them: William Faulkner, Tennessee Williams, Elvis Presley, Miss Eudora Welty, John Grisham, Will D. Campbell, Richard Wright, Oprah Winfrey, Morgan Freeman, Donna Tartt, Beth Henley, Leontyne Price, Ellen Gilchrist, Willie Morris, Barry Hannah, Charley Pride, Muddy Waters, B.B. King, Sela Ward, John Lee Hooker, Mary Ann Mobley, Zig Ziglar, Mary Walker Alexander, Faith Hill, Walker Percy, Tammy Wynette, Craig Claiborne, Rebecca Hill, Robert Johnson, Jimmie Rodgers, Hodding Carter, Shelby Foote, Thomas Harris, Bo Diddley, Jim Henson, James Street, Ray Walston, Archie Manning, Dizzy Dean, Walter Payton, Jerry Rice, Clarence Witherspoon, Steve "Air" McNair, Wesley Walls, W.C. Handy, Charley Conerly, Brett Favre, Lance Alworth, James "Cool Papa" Bell, Sam Cooke, Jerry Clower, Ralph Boston, Red Barber, Nevada Barr, Jimmy Buffet, Anthony Herrera, Johnny Pott, Moe Bandy, D.D. Lewis, Diane Ladd, Ray Perkins, Turner Catledge, Greg Iles, "Son" House, Howlin' Wolf, Stephen Ambrose, Gerald McRaney, Dana Andrews, and Shepard Smith, Fox news anchor. These are just a few of many.

And there are others who came here to hone their skills and share with the world their talents. Some were early settlers who came from the East Coast in search of abundant land and more fertile soil. Settlers and soldiers began their search around Natchez in early 1700. The French explorer Jean-Baptiste Le Moyne, sieur de Bienville, whose brother, Pierre Le Moyne, Sieur d'Iberville, was well known in Louisiana, helped complete Fort Rosalie on the bluffs above the Mississippi River in Natchez in 1716.

This vital land was in demand by Europeans who wanted to expand their holdings, but the land was already occupied by the Natchez Indians. Initially, the Indians and the Frenchmen managed an affable co-existence for more than ten years, until the Indians attacked the fort to reclaim their land in 1729. The Indians killed most of the Frenchmen, but others came later to retaliate and the native Americans were eventually killed or driven away.

More Europeans wanted this prize possession, so over the years the area flew the flags of the French, the English, the Spanish, and finally the U.S. By 1798, Natchez was named capital of the U.S. Territory of Mississippi. Shortly thereafter, a treaty with the Choctaw and Chickasaw Indians opened the old Indian Trail, now the Natchez Trace, which became a wilderness trail linking Natchez with Nashville and other northeastern U.S. destinations.

The Natchez Trace today is a wonderfully undisturbed concrete pathway through the Mississippi countryside. It is peaceful, pretty, and a pleasure to travel, the way highways were meant to be. The speed limit is 50 mph and it is seriously enforced. Look closely, and see deer and wild turkey in the nearby woods.

Back in the day when the historic Natchez Trace was a wilderness trail inhabited by outlaws and hostile natives, settlers began boating down the Mississippi River, coming over to the north and central part of the state from Georgia, the Carolinas, and Virginia. In late 1817, Mississippi was formally admitted to the Union.

Some of the more affluent settlers brought with them their taste for grand homes, which they built with cotton money. Many still stand today and serve as proud vestiges of a time when craftsmanship meant lasting quality. With historic preservation now a major interest in this country, the Deep South is a Mecca for visitors who appreciate heritage treasures and antiques, and Mississippi is a top destination for these pursuits.

Mississippi State Capitol, Jackson. Photo courtesy of Mississippi Development Authority/ Division of Tourism.

NORTH MISSISSIPPI

CORINTH

Corinth is a quiet, historic town in upper northeast Mississippi that once played unwilling host to about 128,000 Federal troops. In May 1862, Federal troops surrounded Corinth in an attempt to capture it. The town's location at the junction of two important railroads made it most important to the Union Army, but the Confederates weren't about to give up easily, so they planned a subterfuge. When General P.G.T. Beauregard learned how out-numbered his Confederate troops were, he ordered a night-time rail evacuation to all points south. When the empty trains arrived to pick up the troops, the Union army was deceived, for General Beauregard's few troops cheered and blew bugles to make it sound as though reinforcements had arrived. The next morning, Union General Hallack found an empty town.

That was one of several encounters between the two armies in Cornith. Another was the bloody Battle of Corinth, when again, the CSA troops were outnumbered. The Corinth National Cemetery holds 5600 graves from that battle and others nearby.

Today the town of about 12,000 has a few pre-Civil War houses on tree-canopied streets and many fine examples of Victorian architecture. A courthouse dominates the town Square, and the state's oldest drug store, Borroum's, is still in the same family and still offers an old-fashioned soda fountain. Their milkshakes are the best!

Borroum's Drug Store, Corinth.

Also in Corinth, see the Black History Museum, with its focus on education and religion, the Curlee House (c. 1857), the Northeast Mississippi Museum, and just outside of town, the Civil War Interpretative Center, a $9 million project of the National Park Service. Big lakes and the Tennessee-Tombigbee Waterway make this area appealing to boaters and fishermen.

94

Elsewhere in North Mississippi closer to Memphis, find **Tunica**, **Lula** and **Robinsonville** and see the casinos now at home there. You'll think you've arrived in Las Vegas without the desert because of the glitz and glitter of shore-docked gambling boats. They want guests to stay to enjoy the name entertainers who regularly perform, so they've put up hotels, restaurants, and all the amenities.

HOLLY SPRINGS

Holly Springs is a must-see if the Old South wields its magic on you. Also built around a town square, Holly Springs has many fine old homes and historic churches. The Marshall County Historical Museum is a good place to start. There's an annual spring Pilgrimage to antebellum homes and a Christmas tour. Most of the homes are listed on the National Register of Historic Places. If you saw the movie, *Cookies Fortune,* with Glenn Close and Liv Tyler, it was filmed here. Holly Springs is about 30 minutes from Memphis.

Literary people are drawn to the region, too, because some of the nation's best writers have called North Mississippi home. Nobel and Pulitzer Prize winner William Faulkner was born in New Albany but spent his formative and adult years in the outstanding town of Oxford, home of the University of Mississippi, the revered Ole Miss.

The Walter Place, Corinth.

OXFORD

Oxford is one of those special places built around a downtown Square, with the Lafayette County Courthouse seeming to hold court over the town. In Faulkner's day, gentlemen sat under the old trees and talked of politics and former times, perhaps they would say better times.

Faulkner's home, Rowan Oak, was his residence from 1930 until his death in 1962. Still on the wall of his study is the handwritten outline of *A Fable,* surviving decades of visitors who've come to see where he lived and worked. Rowan Oak is open by appointment; it is managed by the university.

Back in town, the venerable Ole Miss is a place to see. Founded in 1848 and named by townspeople who hoped the town would have a college as grand as England's Oxford, Ole Miss was occupied by General U.S. Grant in 1862. In fact, legend says that Yankees actually rode their horses inside some of the campus buildings. Also on campus, see the University Museums and a fine collection of Greek and Roman antiquities; also Southern folk art and paintings.

William Faulkner's home Rowan Oak, Oxford.
Photo courtesy of Mississippi Development
Authority/Division of Tourism.

Learn more about the South at the Center for the Study of Southern Culture on campus. It's a well-known research center for most anything Southern. The Ole Miss Blues Archives includes the personal collection of popular bluesman B.B. King, among others. Oxford has great appeal for Ole Miss alums who've "come home" to retire, and on football weekends when the Rebels play home games, tailgating at "The Grove" is the place to be!

TUPELO

Not far away is Tupelo, a three-time All-America City. Tupelo native Elvis Presley became the king of rock n' roll and a world-famous celebrity. Though he died in 1977, fans still come in cars, vans, buses, and motorcycles to see the Elvis Birthplace and Museum. He was born in 1935 in the shotgun house his father built with a bank loan of $180. Sadly, the Presley family was evicted from their neat little house when Elvis was three because they could not re-pay the loan, though they stayed in Tupelo until Elvis was 13, when they moved to Memphis.

The rest is history. The teenager from Tupelo wore long hair, sideburns

Elvis Presley birthplace, Tupelo.

and colorful clothing when other boys wore crew cuts, jeans and T-shirts. But when he sang his mixture of blues, country and spirituals and moved to the music, all else was forgotten. He became an international star; a household name. Those who knew him best say that deep down, Elvis remained a well-mannered, generous country boy who loved his mother and honored his father.

Tupelo is a clean and quiet town known for its high educational standards and devotion to God and country. It's a family town with amenities aplenty including the largest non-metropolitan hospital in the country, the North Mississippi Medical Center. Tupelo is also headquarters for the Natchez Trace, the historic and scenic 444-mile route that links Natchez to Nashville, Tennessee. See exhibits, displays, and a gift shop. Add the Tupelo Auto Museum, the Buffalo Park – where 250 buffalo roam the range – the Gumtree Museum of Art, and see why Tupelo is a choice place to live.

Follow Highway 45 S. to **Aberdeen**, where mansions and magnolias are ready to be photographed. It's a lovely old town with an Episcopal church that has an interesting story. St. John's, built in 1852, boasts a bell sitting atop it that was a gift from 35 New York merchants. The bell is made of silver coin and was sent to the Aberdeen church in 1853. Rumor has it that there was a clergy connection. The church rector and noted author, Joseph Holt Ingraham, had New York friends and associates. When he told his friends about the town and the church, they presented the bell. This and other churches have helped Aberdeen develop a strong sense of community, which Southerners call "a sense of place."

Near Aberdeen, as the crow flies, is **Amory**, once a railroad town and now the home of the annual Amory Railroad Festival. The town is known for its excellent medical community, quiet residential streets, and "Stars Over Amory," a bi-annual extravaganza that attracts Hollywood stars who come to raise money for education. The organizer, a Hollywood agent, hails from Amory. His late mother was a popular teacher, so he decided to start a scholarship in her name. Sam Haskell spearheads the event with his clients and friends in the entertainment industry.

COLUMBUS

The Golden Triangle city of Columbus is a town where antebellum homes are revered. More than 100 pre-Civil War homes and churches adorn the shady streets, and they are indeed fine examples of the architecture of the day. The style is predominantly Greek Revival, though other styles are represented, too. A few are open for tours year 'round, but more are open the first two weeks of April for the Spring Pilgrimage. All the tour homes are on the National Register of Historic Places, and two are National Historic Landmarks.

Throughout this region, the Tennessee-Tombigbee Waterway

winds its way through, creating boating, fishing, and camping opportunities. The Tenn-Tom, as it's called by locals, is America's newest river, a 234-mile long navigational artery that connects middle-America to the Gulf of Mexico; it was built and is managed by the Army Corps of Engineers. It's a treat to see the big yachts "lock through" on their way to Florida and other points south. Fishermen come often for annual tournaments, and they say the big bass are always biting along the Tenn-Tom!

The old plantation chapel on the grounds of Rosewood Manor, Columbus.

Columbus is a progressive city with the US Air Force adding to its progress. Columbus Air Force Base is here; it is one of three USAF pilot training facilities and home to a plethora of military retirees. Columbians are proud of the military connection and equally as proud to be a college town. The nation's oldest state-supported college for women has been here since 1884. The Mississippi University for Women is now co-ed, but there's a strong emphasis on women's studies.

If you love historic homes, Columbus is your town. Grand antebellum mansions and gardens line the streets here, extending a warm welcome to visitors. The difference in Columbus and other towns who host annual Pilgrimages to historic homes is that the homes of Columbus are the residences of local families. They're lived in, cared for, and decorated with fine antiques and art. One such home, Rosewood Manor (c. 1835), sits on four acres of beautifully landscaped grounds and even has a plantation chapel on the premises. Riverview (c. 1852) boasts one of the South's finest examples of decorative molding and is a National Historic Landmark. The outstanding Waverley Plantation is also a National Historic

Waverley Plantation, West Point.

98

Landmark. It has a West Point address, but it's only a few miles from Columbus and it's also a tour home. Some homes are open for tours year 'round, while more are open for the annual spring Pilgrimage. All Columbus tour homes are listed on the National Register and they were all built before1860. Though many homes in the South are on the National Register, few are National Historic Landmarks, which is definitely a mark of distinction.

See the pretty downtown – one of the state's top Main Street programs is here – and stop by the Welcome Center at 300 Main Street. It's hard to miss the yellow and gray Victorian, which was once the Episcopal rectory and the first home of the playwright Tennessee Williams. Columbus's native son was one of the most prolific playwrights ever, and he won Pulitzers for two of his many acclaimed plays, *A Streetcar Named Desire* and *Cat on a Hot Tin Roof.* Early each September, local volunteers present the Tennessee Williams Tribute and Tour, a scholarly and fun event for a long weekend.

The arts have a strong presence downtown, with the fine

Tennessee Williams Welcome Center, Columbus.

CONFEDERATE DECORATION DAY

An event occurred in 1866 that helped to heal the wounds from the recent Civil War. A group of Columbus women met in the home Twelve Gables to plan a way to honor the war dead interred at the Odd Fellows Cemetery. More than 1,000 Confederate soldiers lay in rest, while about 40 Union graves were there, too. They had been wounded on nearby battlefields and transported to homes and churches in Columbus . It was hard to tell blue uniforms from gray in the smoke and confusion of war, and after all, they were all Americans and they needed help, so they were taken to makeshift hospitals near the battlefields.

The women planned a day in April to cut flowers from their gardens to take to the cemetery for what they were calling Confederate Decoration Day. Once there, one of the women saw the neglected and over-grown Union graves, and said to her friends that the "Yankee" soldiers perhaps had wives, mothers, and sisters, too, so she placed a few flowers on the Union graves nearest her. Other ladies followed suit, and soon both Confederate and Union graves were adorned with lovely spring flowers.

Word of this generous gesture by the women of Columbus, spread by word of mouth and finally, a brief mention of it appeared in the *New York Tribune*. Young lawyer F.M. Finch saw the piece and was inspired to write the poem, "The Blue and the Gray." The poem first appeared in the September, 1867, issue of the *Atlantic Monthly* magazine, and after a while, Confederate Decoration Day evolved into the nation's Memorial Day.

Other towns across the South and one in Pennsylvania claim to be the site of the first Memorial Day, though according to the Library of Congress, Columbus, Mississippi, was the only town to honor both Confederate and Union soldiers. The federal soldiers were moved to Shiloh National Cemetery in 1867, though row after row of "Unknown Confederate Soldiers" still rest in peace in what is now Friendship Cemetery in Columbus, where Decoration Day is still observed late each April while the nation's Memorial Day is a May event.

Rosenzweig Arts Center occupying a prominent corner building. Good things happen at the RAC! And each year around the first of May, the huge Market Street Festival is a major event — one of many festive events held in this river city!

Starkville, another of the Golden Triangle cities, is home of the big Mississippi State University, a land grant school that gets multi-millions in research grants. MSU museums and galleries offer endless hours of things to see and do: the Cobb Archaeology Museum, the A.B. McKay Enology Lab — a favorite of wine connoisseurs – the Aquaculture Research Center, the Arboretum, the School of Veterinary Medicine, the Dunn-Seiler Museum, and the John Grisham Room. The best selling novelist Grisham is a MSU alum. Some of these on-campus attractions are open by appointment only.

The third of the Golden Triangle towns is **West Point**, home of the upscale Old Waverly Golf Club and residences, and the magnificent antebellum mansion, Waverley Plantation (c. 1850). Truly a Mississippi showplace, Waverley is a grand Greek Revival structure with an octagonal cupola. It is one of the prestigious National Historic Landmarks, a coveted honor, and it's also on the National Register of Historic Places. Filled with fine antiques, Waverley is open for tours daily. It is the home of the Robert Snow family.

As you venture down to central Mississippi, if you're lucky, you'll pass by the Ole Country Bakery on Hwy. 45 at **Brooksville**, where Mennonite ladies run a bakery and sell the best sweets you'll ever eat, as well as soups and sandwiches for lunch. The Ole Country Bakery is closed Sunday and Monday.

MISSISSIPPI DELTA

Before we reach the central part of the state, there's a special place that's part north and part central but completely unique. It's the mystical Mississippi Delta that runs alongside the mighty Mississippi River. Writer David Cohn once said, "The Mississippi Delta begins in the lobby of the Peabody Hotel in Memphis..." and reaches as far down as Vicksburg. There's no place on earth quite like The Delta, which is what it's called by native Mississippians. It's a land that's rich and poor, deadly quiet and juke joint noisy, sweltering in summer and bitterly cold some winter days. The Delta is laid back and intense, savvy and sleepy, and the rich land is usually covered with

cotton or kudzu. It is the ultimate contradiction. Indeed the Mississippi River is the lifeblood of the land, but tiny backwaters meander through the Delta, sometimes through desolate towns that have a few old stores and not even a stoplight.

The mighty Mississippi River.

No matter, it's a place people love and it has served as inspiration for so many writers, blues musicians, and even a few actors. The actor Morgan Freeman lives in the Delta when he's not on location somewhere; he owns a restaurant in Clarksdale. Jim Henson, creator of the Muppets, Kermit the Frog, Big Bird and other animated characters grew up in the Delta. Learn more about Delta writers and dignitaries in Greenville at the library's Greenville Writers' Exhibit.

GREENVILLE

Greenville is by far the largest town in the Delta. It's the home of the Stein family, who started Steinmart, a favorite shopping place for much of America. Today, it's the music that gets a fair share of attention. Highway 61 is America's undisputed "Blues Highway." The music of bluesmen of international acclaim can be heard throughout this region. A good place to learn more is the Delta Blues Museum in **Clarksdale**, which serves as a repository for blues musicians and their stories. It also contains a life-size wax figure of Muddy Waters and his original cabin from the old Stovall plantation.

Between Clarksdale and **Cleveland**, just off Hwy. 61, detour through the small town of **Alligator**. Alligator sits amicably beside Alligator Lake, a dark and mysterious body of water that looks like a

Louisiana bayou. Knotty cypress knees protrude from the murky depths, inspiring curiosity and more than a modicum of intrigue. **Alligator** was once a thriving town with about 20 stores downtown. Now, it's virtually a ghost town surrounded by rich soil, flat land, and endless cotton fields. Alligator is the home of pioneer television producer Fred Coe (1914 – 1979). As a young man, he left for greener pastures and produced such award-winning movies *as Marty, The Days of Wine and Roses, The Miracle Worker,* and more.

Near **Leland**, between Greenville and Greenwood, is where you'll find the United States Department of Agriculture's largest research facility. The USDA's site at Stoneville has been called the Silicon Valley of Agriculture. The Deer Creek here is where Jim Henson first created such characters as Kermit the Frog.

The Delta Blues Museum, Clarksdale.

GREENWOOD

Greenwood is a Delta border town, along with **Yazoo City**. Greenwood, the state's cotton capital, now sports one of the hottest boutique hotels in the country and it is not close kin to cotton money. It's the upscale Alluvian, a renovated version of the old, abandoned Hotel Irving in downtown Greenwood, and the newly created version is indeed splendid. Expect 45 rooms and five suites of finery, complete with designer *accoutrement*, flat-screen televisions, stainless steel fireplaces, and lush linens. It even has a roof-top terrace reminiscent of big city hotels.

The Alluvian was developed by the president of Greenwood-based Viking Range Corporation to accommodate visiting dignitaries and guests. It is open to the public, and as with most fine, small hotels, it is pricier than rates you'll find at a chain motel, but well worth it to those who don't mind paying for quality. The spa is the best around! My prediction is that downtown Greenwood is on the move, and the Alluvian is the catalyst.

Both Greenwood and Greenville are known to have legendary parties. Delta folks are said to party when the crops are good and when the crops are bad, so they never miss the opportunity. Some of the state's favorite restaurants are in these towns, too, so don't miss the Delta mystique!

DELTA BLUES

Not only does the Mississippi Delta produce bumper crops of cotton, it has produced more prominent blues musicians than any place else on earth. In fact, the blues were born and grew to maturity in the Delta. The amazing thing is that these pure American musicians became popular in Europe long before fans on this side of the Atlantic knew much about blues music. We knew B.B. King, but not many of us knew that "the father of Blues Music" was Robert Johnson. I had not heard the late great Son Thomas sing about..."My baby done got drown-ed," until I moved to north Mississippi. Most of us knew about Muddy Waters, but did we know that his real name is McKinley Morganfield?

My favorite is John Lee Hooker, born in Clarksdale in 1917. His first big hit was "Boogie Chillen", which hit the charts long before he was inducted into the Rock and Roll Hall of Fame. Hooker's music is hypnotic; it's full of raw blues and passion, with no pretense and no artificial polish. In 1989 —at the age of 72— the legendary Hooker paired up with Santana and won his first Grammy for "The Healer." British rocker Eric Clapton, an expert on Hooker's music, emulated Hooker's style as he was developing his own. Others who studied Hooker's music include the Rolling Stones and ZZ Top.

Today, some of the legendary blues clubs have closed, but others have taken their places. Try One Block East in Greenville, the Airport Grocery in Cleveland, Po' Monkey's in Marigold, and the new Ground Zero in Clarksdale, which is owned by the actor Morgan Freeman, who also owns the restaurant Madidi's. Ask locals; they know where the blues can be heard on any given weekend, and if you want to wait for the big Delta Blues festivals and events, there's the Delta Blues Festival in Greenville in September; the new Highway 61 Blues Festival near Greenville in June, and the Sunflower River Blues and Gospel Festival in Clarksdale in August.

Until fairly recently, the Flowing Fountain in Greenville was a sure bet to hear the blues, though it is closed at this writing. Many years ago, a young married couple by the name of Ike and Tina Turner drew a SRO crowd when they appeared there.

The local Blues authority is the Delta Blues Museum in Clarksdale, which began in 1979 for the purpose of preserving and making accessible to the public information, programs, and related services concerning the history and significance of blues music. The old brick walls and wood of the former railroad depot that now houses the museum are perfect for displaying the collection of black and white art, which helps to explain the birth of the blues; see it capsulated below.

"After the Civil War, when the Mississippi Delta was a new frontier, freed African Americans came seeking the opportunities afforded by the rich soil and the timber industry. Black laborers filled the levee camps and were pretty much isolated from the rest of the world. As a result of this isolation, they developed their own music —freely and for the first time— without outside intervention. They remembered the musical traditions from their native Africa and incorporated a form of that sound into their own style. Thus, because of the conditions, the lifestyle, and the land, the blues were born."

Perhaps the best known living blues legend is B.B. King, who, at the age of 80, is about to embark on a world tour to tout his music. Though King and other Delta bluesmen have influenced musicians from the Beatles to Eric Clapton to Stevie Ray Vaughan, King said in a recent interview that the blues do not get much air play today, because radio stations play mostly rock, rap, hip-hop and pop. Others in the business say, however, that the blues have a strong following, and that radio stations seldom play jazz, either, and it's more popular than ever.

       Rolling Stone magazine named B.B. King the third greatest guitarist of all time. Here's something good for the genre and a tribute to B.B. King: at Indianola, his hometown in the Mississippi Delta, plans are underway for the B.B. King Museum and Delta Interpretative Center. This further affirms the fact the Mississippi Delta is the premier place for people who consider the blues a truly unique art form.

B.B. King in concert.
Photo courtesy of
Mississippi Development Authority/
Division of Tourism.

"When you can't turn back the clock, wind it up again."

CENTRAL MISSISSIPPI

VICKSBURG

Vicksburg has that appealing river city ambiance that lets the imagination work overtime. The days of dashing riverboat captains and the landed gentry who booked passage on the paddle wheelers are surely the stuff of novels. Today Vicksburg is home to four permanently docked casinos along the Mississippi River, so there's still a bit of riverboat lore here, though it's of a different kind.

The Delta Queen riverboat on the Mississippi River.
Photo courtesy of Mississippi Development Authority/Division of Tourism.

This river city has its share of historic homes, and an annual Pilgrimage when guests see all the finery. Museums are here, too, and one of the best is the Old Court House Museum in the 1858 building. Exhibited are artifacts, documents and illustrations, and the story of Jefferson Davis launching his political career on the grounds here in 1843.

The Vicksburg Battlefield Museum shows a wonderful collection of early Navy ship models, and they offer a film presentation of *The Vanishing Glory.* The USS Cairo Museum is in an ironclad gunboat sunk during the Civil War, but raised one hundred years later. What an amazing feat. The Cairo is in the 1800-acre Vicksburg National Military Park, the nation's largest after Arlington. With its marble and granite monuments, cannons, and other memories of the 47-day siege and defense of Vicksburg, Civil War buffs, this town is for you.

Some people call Vicksburg "The City of One Hundred Hills," but it could also be called the cave town. When the town was under siege during the Civil War, some local residents sought higher ground away from Yankee cannonballs. They moved their families to the safety of nearby caves for the duration of the siege. One family, the Greens, welcomed a new baby born in a cave, and named him, appropriately, Siege Green.

Statue of Confederate Soldier in Vicksburg National Military Park.

PINEY WOODS COUNTRY LIFE SCHOOL

About 20 miles south of Jackson, the Piney Woods Country Life School is a testament to the dedication of a black educator. Dr. Laurence Jones came to the region in the early 1900s with a Bible and a few dollars to his name. He had a compelling goal: to balance academic knowledge with vocational skills. He started the school in 1909 as a boarding school for economically poor, rural black students.

In the early days, the gifted orator talked himself out of a confrontation with segregationists who thought he was preaching against whites. He even got them to donate money to his cause, the Piney Woods School. Over the years, Dr. Jones old-fashioned teaching philosophy has proved to be so successful other schools have used it a model. Dr. Jones died in 1975; he was 93.

The school is still going strong today. The beautiful campus and museum honors Dr. Jones and his leadership and encourages tours of the school and impressive grounds, including five lakes and fertile farmland. See it on Highway 49 in the Piney Woods community.

JACKSON

The largest city and the state's capital, Jackson, is in central Mississippi. Jackson, a place that evokes pride in native Mississippians, has an irrepressible spirit. It was burned during the Civil War to the extent that nothing was left but a few chimneys, thus the moniker "Chimneyville." Jackson reinvented itself, stronger and better than ever, and its accomplishments are myriad. The Mississippi Legislature passed one of the first laws in the English speaking world that protected the rights of married women.

106

Today, Jackson is a major medical center for the state. The world's first kidney autotransplant was performed at University Medical Center in 1962, and the world's first human lung transplant was performed at UMC in 1963. A good place to get a feel for the state is in the hallowed halls of the old capitol building. It is a place of reverence for Mississippians, since so much of the state's early history took place inside this grand Greek Revival structure. It was the capitol from 1939 until 1903, and now it serves the state well as the Mississippi State Historical Museum.

The Mississippi Museum of Art is downtown, with traveling and permanent exhibits. It houses the world's largest collection of work by Mississippi artists, as well it should. Other museums and galleries are here, too, and the seat of government always deserves a closer look.

The Ag Museum (actually the Mississippi Agriculture and Forestry/National Aviation Museum) presents another good look at perhaps the best of Mississippi: its rural roots. This living history museum includes a general store in Small Town, Mississippi, where old-fashioned candy, toys, and souvenirs can be purchased; a 1920s era farm, and a huge exhibit building that houses

The Craft Center at The Ag Museum, Jackson
Photo courtesy of
Mississippi Development Authority
Division of Tourism

crop-duster airplanes and other key factors in the state's agricultural heritage. This museum is a family favorite! The 40-acre Ag Museum includes the Heritage Center, a crafts gallery, a restaurant, and a rose garden.

Nearby is the Mississippi Music Hall of Fame. At home here are exhibits of Elvis Presley, B.B. King, Conway Twitty, Robert Johnson, Leontyne Price, among many. The Mississippi Sports Hall of Fame and Museum honors the state's sports heroes, and they are legion in this futuristic complex.

Enjoy the excellent restaurants that serve a variety of food from down home cookin' to ethnic food to sophisticated cuisine. That's a good thing about Jackson. Most anything you require is never too far away.

Near Jackson is **Canton**, where a pre-Civil War courthouse serves as an anchor for the town. It is one of the few old courthouses left intact and unaltered. You saw it if you saw the film based on

John Grisham's book, *A Time to Kill.*

Northeast of Jackson find **Philadelphia**, a town that had its share of publicity during the Civil Rights era, though Philadelphians today are quick to say that all that activity is a thing of the past. Philadelphia is a pretty town with friendly people who are pleased to invite visitors to the stellar Neshoba County Fair –an authentic, old, camp town fair— and the Choctaw Indian Fair, two popular events held each summer.

Camphouses at Neshoba County Fair, Philadelphia.
Photo courtesy of
Philadelphia Chamber of Commerce.

Choctaw, Mississippi, near Philadelphia, is where the Choctaw Indian Tribe, under the astute and visionary leadership of Chief Phillip Martin, runs several successful businesses. Among them are six manufacturing companies, two casinos, several restaurants, two hotels, two major golf courses and a 120-bed tribal member nursing home. The Choctaws have done themselves proud with these properties.

Choctaw Indian Chief Pushmataha.
Photo courtesy of
Mississippi Department of
Archives and History

The Dentzel Carousel, Meridian.
Photo courtesy of Meridian Convention and Visitors Bureau.

MERIDIAN

Meridian is next. For a town that was burned to the ground by the Union Army and declared by a military officer as "...no longer existing," Meridian could tell the nation a thing or two about growth. The city re-built itself with gusto, and thanks to trains, planes and highways, it continues to grow and prosper. Interstate highways I-20 and I-59 join in Meridian, and businesses love having access to the travel trade.

Things to see and do in Meridian include the Dentzel Carousel (c. 1890) at Highland Park, the world's only two-row stationary Dentzel menagerie. It is a National Historic Landmark. And speaking of carousels, local and regional artists have created carousel horses now placed in prominent positions around town. Nearby is the Jimmie Rodgers Museum where memorabilia is displayed that designates Rodgers as "the father of country music." The American music legend was born in Meridian, as were the Key Brothers. See a pictorial tribute to the brothers who set a world flight endurance record in 1935.

Jimmy Rodgers,
"The Singing Brakeman."
Photo courtesy of Meridian
Convention and Visitors Bureau.

Something new and grand has the town talking. Mississippi State

University purchased the old Grand Opera House and the Marks-Rothenberg store and a renovation is underway. Set to officially open in late summer 2006, the two historic sites will become The Riley Center. The opera house will host performances throughout the year, and the Marks-Rothenberg Center will be the home of the new Meridian convention center. This will be a terrific asset to downtown Meridian.

Causeyville General Store, Causeyville.
Photo courtesy of
Meridian Convention and Visitors Bureau.

Two historic homes are tourable, Merrehope (antebellum) and the Frank W. Williams Home (Victorian). South of Meridian off I-59 is Dunn's Falls on the Chunky River, site of a gristmill and waterfall, and great photo opportunities. The old Causeyville General Store on Hwy. 19 S. is a step-back in time to 1895. It is about as authentic as it gets, and it even has a gristmill.

Having been a lifelong fan of gypsy lore, this story holds particular interest for me. Here's the story … for some unknown reason, one Kelly Mitchell, the reputed Queen of the Gypsies, appeared in Meridian around 1915. She died here, was laid in state for more than a week as the gypsy tribe gathered to pay respects, then laid to rest at Rose Hill Cemetery. Enroute

Dunn's Falls near Meridian.

to the cemetery, according to printed accounts, about 5,000 gypsies followed the hearse. Her husband, gypsy King Emil Mitchell, later chose to be buried beside his wife at Rose Hill. Today, there appears to be a steady stream of family members visiting the graves of the gypsy royalty, for gifts of fruit and juices are sometimes left in honor of the dearly departed, or perhaps for the next visitor.

Meridian is also the home of Peavey Electronics, thought to be the world's largest manufacturer of musical sound systems and amplification equipment. Such masters of the guitar as Eddie Van Halen are said to endorse Peavy products, which began in the early 1960s in the basement of founder Hartley Peavey.

HISTORIC PRESERVATION

In the Deep South, historic preservation has many monikers. Some towns use the term for downtown development; others use it when a single house is restored. Or the restoration project could be a water tower, an old bridge, or a dilapidated opera house. Usually in these three Southern states, historic preservation often refers to a house, preferably an antebellum, meaning "before the war," and in this case, the Civil War. The consensus is that we lose our sense of place when we lose our landmarks; therefore we make every effort to save them. Sense of place is important to Southerners for it's all about who we are.

Back in the 1930s, a federal government office decided to document noteworthy buildings across the country through what they called the Historic American Buildings Survey (HABS). The results of the survey gave preservationists an inkling of what needed preserving, and to some the impetus to start.

After the Civil War and Reconstruction and because of a lack of money for maintenance, many old houses in the South were by then peeling and reeling. World War I, the Great Depression, and World War II were continued impediments to preservation efforts. Unfortunately by the 1960's when preservation was again taken seriously, so many of the treasures were by then lost, either from neglect or to development. Natchez, however, did a better job of salvaging what they had, and they in turn started the first Pilgrimage in the mid-South.

People came to see the homes of history during the early Pilgrimages, and they apparently loved what they saw; architectural grace and grandeur. Since, in the early to mid-1800's, architects were scarce in some of the South's remote regions, skilled craftsmen used pattern books instead of original plans.

And still they come today. They look up at the tall columns and wonder how they were so carefully crafted and then placed so securely without cranes and power tools. The columns represent the Greek Revival style, which was the most widespread and popular architectural style of the mid-1800s. The opulent style was not entirely for show, though many of the planters and others who built them wanted to show their wealth. There was often a utilitarian reason for the recessed porches and thick columns and pediments, and that reason was comfort. Such design features provided shade from the hot Southern sun.

Thanks to preservationists and those who promote heritage tourism, the South is now holding on to what's left. Historic foundations are springing up in many towns and cities, and they're serious about the work they've undertaken, which, we hope, is restoring the properties to their original state. There's something sad about a lovely old home that is nothing but a shell of what it once was. Modern conveniences are fine and we're all spoiled for them, but we hope they aren't at the expense of the integrity of a marvelous old mansions, lovingly built so long ago.

SOUTH MISSISSIPPI AND THE GULF COAST

This region of the state has its own personality, perhaps one that dates back to the early settlers who came to the piney woods and magnolia-scented hills of Natchez looking for a place to call home. Some of the settlers in the eastern part were once called "stubborn" because they wanted no part of a war that they believed served the plantation system. In fact, at the outbreak of the Civil War, Jones County seceded from the state when the state seceded from the Union, thus was born "The Free State of Jones." The eastern counties of Wayne, Jones, Jasper, Forrest, Smith, Covington, Perry and Greene were more interested in timber than farming, so big cotton growing farms were scarce. Plantations flourished around Natchez, however, and it was cotton money that built the grand mansions still in abundance today.

With the arrival of the lumber barons from elsewhere in the country, gone was the pioneer spirit of the piney woods people. The region lost most of its virgin timber in the late 1800s; men left their land to work in the mills, and the culture of the region began to change. Where tall pines and hardwood once grew wild and free, mud holes and barren land replaced the towering trees.

Today a little of the pioneer spirit remains, but it has been somewhat influenced by neighbors New Orleans and Mobile. As a product of South Mississippi, I grew up reading the New Orleans *Times-Picayune* and the Mobile *Press Register*, along with the hometown paper, the *Laurel Leader-Call.* Unbeknownst at the time, I was well informed for a buck-toothed country girl who had rather read than eat. And yes, though I've been away for most of my adult life, I still call South Mississippi 'home.'

NATCHEZ

The grandeur of Natchez is incomparable. It's a city built on the bluff of the Mississippi River, and it once had more millionaires, per capita, than any other city in the country. That was back in the early to mid-1800s, when cotton was king and shipped to world markets via the river. The homes built by cotton money still stand tall and proud in this old river city, where about 500 historic structures give visitors plenty to see.

Natchez, founded in 1817, is the undisputed *grande dame* of the South, but it also has its wild side. There's the quiet aristocracy found in the grand old homes on the hill, and there's a bit of frontier bawdiness that was known to be the norm at Natchez Under the Hill. In its heyday, Under the Hill was where the ladies of the night, not the ladies of the town, were found; it was sometimes referred to as "The Barbary Coast of Mississippi." It's where the riverboat gamblers, frontiersmen, and renegades congregated. Today, Under the Hill is a place where restaurants, gift shops, and a permanently docked casino are found.

The Delta Queen and the Mississippi Queen still dock here often, but gone are the days of lawlessness. Passengers on these riverboats come to the see the homes of history, and judging from the oohhs and aahhs, they are not disappointed. Natchez is a Pilgrimage town, actually they started the major historic home event in 1932. After all, this town has the largest number of pre-Civil War structures in the U.S., according to the research I've seen, so they should have begun the tradition. The two Natchez Pilgrimages run a month each Spring and two weeks each fall, and both events feature costumed hostesses in big hoop skirts, just as though they stepped out of the 19th century.

The Mississippi Queen and Delta Queen moored at Natchez.

Perhaps the most interesting tour home in Natchez is Longwood, a Moorish-style mansion still unfinished on the interior, because the workmen who were building it left at the outset of the Civil War. They went home to Pennsylvania to join the Union forces. After the war, the money was gone and the homeowner had died. Noted architect Samuel Sloan of Philadelphia designed Longwood as the 32-room showplace for the very rich Dr. Haller Nutt and his family. Dr. Nutt was a Yankee sympathizer, though his affinity for the Union army did not prevent them from burning his cotton fields in Mississippi and Louisiana, said to be valued at more than $3 million, a princely sum in the day.

Dr. Nutt's family continued to live at Longwood in the huge, cool, finished, multi-room basement until 1968. It is truly amazing to see the architectural details in this stage of building. Tools and instruments are still left as they were around 1861.

One of the grandest of the grand anywhere is Stanton Hall (c. 1857), perhaps the most photographed home in the country. It has graced so many magazine covers, one loses count. It occupies an entire city block, and on the premises is the fine restaurant, The Carriage House. The century-old live oak trees that surround the house and property are nothing short of amazing.

Longwood and Stanton Hall are National Historic Landmarks, Pilgrimage tour homes and owned by the Natchez Pilgrimage Garden Club.

Longwood (c. 1860-61), and unfihisned showplace, Natchez.
Photo courtesy of Mississippi Development Authority/ Division of Tourism.

Other magnificent mansions that are favorites of mine are Dunleith, Monmouth –both of which boast fabulous restaurants and are B&B inns – Choctaw, Rosalie, Mount Repose, and Melrose. Beautiful churches abound here, and the downtown area is a shoppers delight.

North of Natchez is historic Jefferson College in **Washington**, the school that existed from 1811- 1964. Further north, **Port Gibson** awaits, another town with lovely old homes. In the vicinity, find the haunting Ruins of Windsor, the tall towers being all that remain of the state's largest home, built c. 1859, burned in 1890, except for the 23 fluted columns.

Do you remember seeing the film "Raintree County" with Elizabeth Taylor and Montgomery Clift? The tall columns in that film are the Ruins of Windsor.

The Ruins of Windsor near Port Gibson.
Photo courtesy of
Mississippi Development Authority/
Division of Tourism.

LAUREL

Drive through clean and green small towns and arrive in Laurel, which boasts one of the prettiest streets in the South, Fifth Avenue. On a corner of Fifth Avenue, a couple of blocks from downtown, find the outstanding Lauren Rogers Museum of Art. It is most unusual to see such a quality museum outside an urban area, but here it is. The Georgian Revival-style museum began in 1923 with the design by Rathbone deBuys of New Orleans and the interior done by the Chicago firm of Watson and Walton. The museum was established to honor its namesake, young newlywed Lauren Eastman Rogers, who died in 1922 following an appendectomy. His parents set up the endowment for the museum, which was to have been his home.

Lauren Rogers Museum, Laurel.

Enter, and be impressed. The collections include Indian basketry, Japanese woodblock prints, Georgian silver, and a permanent collection of paintings by major American and European artists of the 19th and 20th centuries, among them Winslow Homer. There's an extensive reference library and a great gift shop.

Laurel's leading industry a few years back was related to lumber, for the Masonite Corporation was founded and located here. Then came the oil boom, and now it's a combination of industry and business that keeps the town afloat.

HATTIESBURG

Hattiesburg was once over-shadowed by neighbor Laurel, now it's a city that's forged a name for itself as one of the most progressive cities in the state. Hattiesburg is the hub of activity for this part of the state, and the home of the sprawling University of Southern Mississippi, called simply "Southern" in these parts. This big university is one of the best-known in the South and it has superb on-campus amenities. The USM Museum of Art is here, where the work of Mississippi artists Walter Anderson and Marie Hull can be seen, among other Southern artists.

The de Grummond Children's Literature Collection at the

McCain Library and Archives boasts 55,000 volumes in the collection, including 200 versions of *Cinderella* and 150 versions of *Little Red Riding Hood.* The collection holds a very rare edition of Aesop's *Fables,* published in 1530.

Hattiesburg is coastal in attitude, but the real thing is not too far away. The Mississippi Gulf Coast offers a plethora of big hotels, fine restaurants, and a dozen or so casinos that are Mississippi's answer to Las Vegas. More than that, however, "the Coast," as native Mississippians call it, is a 55-mile stretch of waterfront along the heel of the state, with 26 of those miles sporting white sand beaches perfect for strolling, kayaking, swimming, or parasailing.

NATCHEZ -- THE SOCIAL CENTER

Even while outlaw gangs and bandits robbed and sometimes murdered travelers on the nearby overland route now known as the Natchez Trace, citizens of early Natchez were far removed from the rough trade of the "wilderness." Natchez was a place of culture and refined entertainment, of formal dinners and parties that sometimes lasted the weekend. "Social elegance" was the term preferred by Natchezians. The newly organized Natchez Theatrical Association constructed a new brick building to house 700 patrons and hired a resident director in 1828. One year later, this country's foremost Shakespearean actor, Edwin Forrest, introduced *Hamlet* to a full house. Other great actors came and went, including Jenny Lind. Because of Lind's popularity and the curiosity she generated, the venue was moved to the Methodist Church, which had a seating capacity of 800.

About this time, a Natchez native was making a name for herself throughout the country and in Europe, but perhaps not in her hometown. She studied in Europe in the 1850s and acquired quite a following there. The former slave with the amazing voice used the stage name, "The Black Swan," and enthralled the Queen of England and her guests at a command performance.

Natchez continued to be a popular gathering place for dignitaries and others who had social, political and literary aspirations. One resident of Natchez was perhaps the most prolific writer of his day. Born in Maine in 1809, young Joseph Holt Ingraham became a professor of languages at Jefferson College near Natchez around 1831. In 1832, he married a Natchez planter's daughter and began a writing career with the publishing of *The Southwest: By a Yankee* in 1835. His wife introduced him to the Episcopal Church; he became an Episcopalian, later a priest, and continued to write. His books were not critically acclaimed by critics and other writers, but they sold. He was, in fact, one of the first writers to dramatize the life of Christ. Ingraham was a scholar and an intellectual.

After serving at St. John's in Aberdeen and other parishes in the South, he went to Holly Springs as rector and continued to write. Among his published works was *The Prince of the House of David.* Amid a beginning war, financial difficulties and problems with publishers, Ingraham shot himself in his church office in Holly Springs. The year was 1860; he was 51. The family denied suicide and the community believed that the shot was accidental, but the mystery lived long after his death. And his books continued to be sold.

THE MISSISSIPPI GULF COAST

BILOXI/GULFPORT

The Coast's largest towns are Biloxi and Gulfport, which run together and blend amicably. The historic Biloxi Lighthouse has guided ships to safe harbor since 1848. Look to these attractions to learn more about the region: The J.L. Scott Marine Education Center and Museum has a 44,000-gallon tank aquarium and live animals native to the coastal area. The Maritime and Seafood Industry Museum houses coastal photographs, artifacts, and a film on hurricane devastation. The Marine Life Oceanarium in Gulfport features underwater dive shows, a dolphin and sea lion show, and more.

Overlooking the Gulf is Beauvoir, the last home and presidential library of Jefferson Davis, President of the Confederate States of America. A museum and gift shop is on the premises. Luckily, the grand and historic Beauvoir survived the deadly Hurricane Camille, said to have been the worst storm in U.S. history. The hurricane hit the coast on August 17, 1969, with its 205-mile per hour winds and waves up to 20 feet high. The storm killed 129 Mississippians, destroyed more than 3,000 homes along the coast, damaged another 48,000, and destroyed 568 Mississippi businesses. Even Hattiesburg, 70 miles north, experienced 140-mile per hour winds. This storm will never be forgotten by coastal residents, who've experienced their share of hurricanes.

Jefferson Davis' home "Beauvoir," Biloxi.
Photo courtesy of Mississippi Development Authority/Division of Tourism.
Unfortunately, Beauvoir was heavily damaged by hurricane Katrina.

The Biloxi Mardi Gras Museum offers a good look at colorful costumes and memorabilia. It is located in an historic hotel. Yes, Mardi Gras is celebrated here, too, for like neighbor New Orleans, people love an excuse to have a good time.

Soon to be in Biloxi is the Ohr-O'Keefe Museum, designed by Frank Gehry and celebrating the work of George Ohr, the self-proclaimed "Mad Potter of Biloxi." Inside the museum, find the world's largest collection of Ohr's unusual pottery. His work is now almost impossible to find and afford.

Biloxi Bay Charters and Nature Tours are favorites of families, for the eco-tours include picnicking, fishing, swimming and exploring on the south side of Deer Island, a barrier island. Take the Ship Island Ferry out of Gulfport to another barrier island, and learn about the offshore islands and their importance to the main land.

It is a pleasure to drive along the Coast highway, U.S. Highway 90, between **Bay St. Louis** and **Long Beach**, for it's a tree-canopied boulevard with great beachfront houses on one side and the Gulf on the other. Bay St. Louis' "Old Town" is a haven for collectors of Mississippi art, artists, and antiques. The Library here is now a National Literary Landmark in honor of Stephen Ambrose, who often researched his books here. If you remember seeing the film *This Property is Condemned*, starring Natalie Wood and Robert Redford in younger years, you may recognize the Bay St. Louis Depot, for it served as the centerpiece in the 1966 film written by Mississippian Tennessee Williams.

Ocean Springs is the location of the Gulf Islands National Seashore Visitors Center; it's an interpretive center for the coastal region. Shearwater Pottery is here, and so is the Walter Anderson Museum of Art. Anderson was a native artist with a national following.

Anywhere on the Coast and especially at the several casino buffett tables, you're never too far from excellent seafood and all sorts of fun! Some say they came for a visit and stayed a lifetime.

The Beau Rivage Resort and Casino, one of ten Gulf Coast casinos, boasts 1740 guest rooms, twelve restaurants, several specialty shops and a 76,000 square foot gaming area. Recently recognized as one of the top 500 hotels in the world, the Beau Rivage also features a 31 slip marina, a spa and will open the Tom Fazio designed Fallen Oak golf course in 2006.

The historic Biloxi Lighthouse, a cast-iron land-mark standing 65-feet tall and built in 1848, is a favorite of locals and visitors alike. A distinction of the lighthouse is its several female lightkeepers, including Maria Younghans, who tended the light for 53 years.

Photo by Sylvia Higginbotham.

Still in South Mississippi though not the Coast, the antebellum Rosalie (c. 1823) in Natchez has a rich and colorful history. During the Civil War when Natchez was occu-pied by Federal troops, Rosalie became the confiscated headquarters of Union Army General Ulysses S. Grant. Today, it is owned by the Mississippi Society of the Daughters of the American Revolution. The DAR has preserved as many original fur-nishings as possible and Rosalie once again welcoming guests. Rosalie is open for tours. A gift shop is on the premises.

MISSISSIPPI RECIPES

Mississippi is a hospitable state where food is appreciated and enjoyed, and is a big part of most every memorable event: wedding receptions, christenings, family gatherings after funerals, family reunions, supper clubs, tailgate parties, business functions, what have you! Superb cooks live here, and universities are now teaching culinary arts to up and coming Southern chefs, among the best is Mississippi University for Women in Columbus where chefs in training learn from the professionals.

Hauté cuisine is indeed available in the Magnolia State, but many natives still love their soul food. In fact, we hear that soulful Southern cooking is making a come-back and "soul food suppers" are especially big in urban areas where Southern people congregate. The expected dishes are greens – turnips, collards, or mustard – always served with Trappey's Pepper in vinegar, or Bruce's pepper sauce, a bowl of "pot-likker," sweet potatoes, black-eyed peas, fresh corn, sliced vine-ripened tomatoes, fresh green onions, various salads, deviled eggs, a hot pone of cornbread, and great country food is about to be enjoyed. Country cookin' extraordinaire!

Some of our Mississippi recipes came from one of the best and prettiest cookbooks in the South, *A Grand Heritage: A Culinary Legacy of Columbus, MS.* If you want to order it, contact us (address in back) and we'll pass the information along to the publishers. Thanks to friends Juliaette Sharp and Linda Rood for use of a few of their recipes.

CHEESE MOLD WITH STRAWBERRY PRESERVES

1 lb. medium Cheddar cheese shredded
4 green onions and tops, chopped
Mayonnaise
1/2 cup pecans, chopped
1 (8 oz.) jar strawberry preserves
Round butter crackers

Mix together softened cheese, onion, and enough mayonnaise to hold mixture together, adding one teaspoon at a time. Add nuts; shape mixture into a ring on a tray and chill. Before serving, fill center of ring with strawberry preserves and serve with round butter crackers. Serves 12.

SPINACH DIP

1 cup dairy sour cream
1 cup mayonnaise
1 can water chestnuts,
chopped
1 (10 oz.) pkg. frozen chopped spinach

3 to 4 green onions, chopped
1 pkg. Swiss vegetable soup mix

Cook spinach and drain well. Mix all ingredients well and chill three to four hours. Better if made day ahead. Serve with Melba toast rounds or wheat thins.

ITALIAN SURPRISE

1 lb. ground beef
1 lb. hot sausage
1 lb. Velveeta cheese

1/2 cup pizza sauce
1 teasp. oregano

Cook and drain beef and sausage. Mix in the cheese, pizza sauce and oregano. Spread on two loaves of party rye bread. Bake 10-15 minutes at 425°.

CHIPPED BEEF BALL

1 (8 oz.) pkg. cream cheese
(room temperature)
1 (2-1/2 oz.) jar dried beef,
finely chopped
3 green onion tops, finely chopped

2 tabsp. pickle relish

Party crackers

In a bowl cream together the cream cheese and one half of the chipped beef. Add the green onion and pickle relish and mix well. Chill the mixture for one hour in a round container. Remove the ball from the container and roll it in the remainder of the chipped beef. Allow the ball to stand at room temperature for 30 minutes. Serve the beef ball with crackers.

CREAM CHEESE FAVORITE

Unwrap a block of Cream Cheese, place on a nice tray. Top with Mint Jelly or Picapepper sauce. Place Ritz or party crackers on tray with a festive serving knife.

CAULIFLOWER DIP

1 cup mayonnaise
1 (8 oz.) carton sour cream
2 teasp. celery seed

1 (6 oz.) pkg. garlic salad
    dressing mix
Cauliflower florets

Combine first four ingredients in a bowl. Refrigerate for 24 hours. Serve dip with cauliflower florets (or other fresh vegetable). Makes about one pint.

SMOKED OYSTER DIP

1 (8 oz.) pkg. cream cheese
    (room temperature)
1 (4 oz.) can chopped black
    olives, drained
2 (3-3/4 oz.) cans smoked
    oysters, drained and chopped

1-1/2 cups mayonnaise
Several dashes Tabasco
3 teasp. lemon juice
Wheat thins

Combine the first six ingredients in a bowl; chill. Serve with wheat thins or Melba toast. Makes about two cups.

BEST BEAN SALAD

4 cans Blue Lake beans,
    drained
3 med. white onions, cut in
    rings
3 jars artichoke hearts

Celery, tender part, diced
2 cans water chestnut, sliced
Wishbone salad dressing

Mix first five ingredients. Let stand. Just before serving, add salad dressing.

CONGEALED FRUIT SALAD

2 (3 oz.) pkgs. strawberry
  Jell-o
1 (12 oz.) can pineapple
1 (#2 can) sweet dark cherries

1 (8 oz.) pkg. cream cheese,
  softened
1 (12 oz.) can Coca Cola

Drain the pineapple and cherries; save juice and heat to boiling. Pour over Jell-O and stir until dissolved. Cool. Cream softened cheese with cola and add cherries and pineapple. Stir mixture into Jell-O. Pour into mold and chill until firm, or in Pyrex dish to serve on salad plates covered with crisp lettuce.

CORN SALAD

3 (12 oz.) cans shoe peg corn
1 cup bell peppers, chopped
1/2 cup green onions, chopped

1 (6 oz.) bottle salad olives
1 (8 oz.) bottle Italian dressing

Mix all ingredients and marinate at least eight hours. Will keep well in refrigerator for several days. Serves 16.

PINEAPPLE ICE CREAM SALAD

1 pkg. lime or other flavored
  Jell-o
1 cup boiling water
1 pint vanilla ice cream

1 cup crushed pineapple
1 cup chopped nuts, optional

Dissolve Jell-O in boiling water; add ice cream and stir until dissolved. Mix in pineapple and nuts. Chill until firm; serve on lettuce beds. Serves 4- 6.

TURNIP GREENS

Buy about 2-1/2 pounds fresh turnip greens. Cut off hard stems and wash thoroughly, four or five times. In a large Dutch oven or pot place 1/4 pound of salt pork and fill half full with water. Add the washed greens and cook for about an hour, or until greens are tender. When nearly done, add salt to taste and one teaspoon of sugar. With two knives, chop cooked turnips before serving.

NOTE: *Some urban cooks use cans of 'Allen's Turnip Greens, Southern Style.' Add several sliced turnip roots, ham or bacon, salt, and a pinch of sugar. Tasty and easy!*

STRING BEANS WITH ALMONDS

1 can string beans	2 tabsp. almonds
1 small can mushrooms	2 tabsp. butter

Cook beans according to directions; drain most of liquid. Sauté almonds and mushrooms in butter, add to beans. Serves 4.

POTATOES AU GRATIN

4 cups cooked, cubed potatoes	2 cups med. white sauce
1 small onion, chopped	1 cup grated cheese
2 tabsp. pimento, chopped	Cracker crumbs

Sauté onion in butter until tender. Add potatoes, pimento, salt and pepper to taste. Mix with white sauce and pour in pan. Sprinkle cheese and one-fourth cup buttered cracker crumbs over top. Bake 20 minutes in moderate oven. Serves 6.

COPPER CARROTS
Excellent for picnics or tailgating!

2 lbs. carrots, sliced cross-
    wise and par-boiled.
1 med. green pepper, sliced
    crosswise
1 onion, sliced crosswise
1 can tomato soup
1/2 cup salad oil

1 cup sugar
3/4 cup vinegar
1 teasp. dry mustard
Salt and pepper to taste
1/2 teasp Worchesteshire

    Mix all ingredients and marinate overnight. Keeps several days in refrigerator. Use as a side dish or appetizer, with toothpicks.

EGGPLANT CASSEROLE

1 medium eggplant
1 cup sliced onion
2 cups chopped celery
1 egg, beaten
1/4 cup butter

1-1/2 cups grated sharp
    Cheddar cheese
2 slices bread, no crust
Salt and pepper to taste
Butter for top

    Peel and chop eggplant. Place in a sauce pan, add onion and celery. Cover vegetables with water and cook until tender; drain well. Place in bowl; add beaten egg, one-fourth cup melted butter, one cup cheese and bread, which has been torn into small pieces. Place all in a buttered casserole and sprinkle top with remaining cheese and dot with butter. Bake at 325° for 30 minutes, or until set. Serves 8.

CREAMY SQUASH

3 cups cooked squash
2 tabsp. grated onion
1 teasp. salt
I cup dairy sour cream

1/2 tabsp. dill weed
Pepper to taste
Dash of celery salt

    Boil squash and onion in salted water until tender; drain, mix with sour cream; add seasonings. Put in buttered casserole, sprinkle with celery salt. Heat at 350° until bubbly, about 20 minutes. Serves 6 – 8.

BROTHER'S FAVORITE BROCCOLI

1 pkg. frozen, chopped
  broccoli
1 med. onion, chopped
1 stick butter
1 jar Cheese Whiz with jalapeno

1 can cream of chicken soup
1/2 soup can milk
1/2 cup cooked rice
1/4 cup slivered almonds

Cook broccoli by directions on package; drain well. Sauté onion in butter. Add Cheese Whiz, soup, milk, and rice. Mix all ingredients well. Pour into greased casserole dish and top with slivered almonds. Bake in 350° oven for 30 minutes.

CHICKEN SUPREME

6 chicken breasts
1 can mushroom soup

2 cloves garlic
1 pkg. English peas, frozen

Salt and pepper chicken, dredge in flour, then brown in hot fat. Place in casserole. Mince garlic and add to mushroom soup that has been diluted with one-half can water. Pour over chicken and bake at 350° for 45 minutes. Add peas and bake until peas are done. Serve over hot cooked rice. Serves 6.

SPECIAL SEAFOOD CASSEROLE

1/2 cup chopped each green
  pepper, onion, and celery
1/2 cup butter
2/3 cup flour
1/2 teasp. minced garlic
1/2 teasp. salt
Dash of red pepper

1/4 teasp. paprika
1 (10-3/4 oz.) can cream of
  mushroom or cream shrimp
  soup
2 cups milk
6 oz. crab meat, fresh or frozen
12 oz. frozen shrimp

Sauté first three ingredients in butter. Stir in flour; cook about one minute; add seasonings. Stir in soup and milk and cook over medium heat until thickened. Layer crab meat and shrimp in casserole, top with grated cheese and bake at 350° for about 30 minutes. Serves 6.

BAKED PORK CHOPS

6 (1-1/2 inch thick) pork
  chops
3 tart apples, cored and
  sliced
1/4 cup brown sugar

1/4 teasp. white sugar
2 tabsp. butter

Arrange pork chops in single layer in oven dish or pan. Cover with sliced apples; sprinkle apples with sugars and dot with butter. Cover and bake at 375° for about 1-1/2 hours. Serves 6.

ROAST LEG OF LAMB

5 to 6 lb. leg of lamb
Garlic, sliced crosswise

Mint jelly

Puncture lamb with a sharp skewer in six places; insert think slices of garlic in each puncture. Baked uncovered in a 475° oven for 30 minutes. Reduce heat to 325° and roast, allowing 20 minutes per pound (medium). Slice and serve with mint jelly.

MISSISSIPPI CATFISH STEW

2 lbs. catfish fillets
1/2 cup chopped bacon
1 cup chopped onion
2 (1 lb., 13 oz.) cans
  tomatoes
2 cups diced potatoes, par-boiled

1 cup catsup
2 tabsp. Worcestershire
2 teasp. salt
Pepper to taste, black or
  red (cayenne)

Remove skin from fillets; cut into one-inch pieces. In large skillet fry bacon until done; add onion and cook until tender. Add tomatoes, potatoes, catsup and seasonings. Heat to boiling; reduce heat and cook, covered, for about 30 minutes, stirring occasionally. Add fish and continue cooking for another 25 - 30 minutes, until potatoes are tender. Stir gently on occasion. Serves 6.

NOTE: Catfish stew, fried catfish, or steak is a good river house meal served on the deck with freshly made cole slaw, garden vegetable tray, baked beans and hushpuppies. Making home-made ice cream to serve at sunset makes it a special treat!

KEY LIME PIE

4 eggs   1/3 cup lime or lemon juice
1 can condensed milk   Baked pie shell

Separate whites and yolks of eggs. Beat the yolks of four eggs and the white of one until thick. Add the condensed milk and beat again. Add lime juice and stir until thick. Fold in the three remaining egg whites, which have been beaten until dry. Pour into baked pie shell and cook in slow oven (250°-300°) for 15 minutes.

BAKED APPLES

4 baking apples, cored   1/2 cup apple cider
4 tablespoons maple syrup   Ground cinnamon

Peel one inch from tops of apples. Place apples in a microwave-safe casserole dish. Pour cider around them. Fill each apple with one tablespoon syrup. Dust lightly with cinnamon. Cover and microwave on high for ten minutes or until fork tender. Serves 4.

BREAD PUDDING WITH PINEAPPLE

1 cup sugar   1 lg. can evaporated milk
3/4 stick butter   1 lg. can crushed pineapple
3 eggs, beaten   5 cups bread crumbs, chunks

Preheat oven to 375°. Mix sugar and butter in large bowl. Add eggs, evaporated milk, and pineapple. Mix well; stir in bread crumbs. Place in two-quart baking dish and bake for about 35 minutes. Serves 8.

OLD-FASHIONED GARDEN WEDDING CAKE
Great anytime…not just for a wedding!

1 cup butter (2 sticks),
  softened
3 cups sugar
4 cups cake flour
1 teasp. baking soda
2 teasps. baking powder
1/4 teasp. salt

2 cups buttermilk
1 teasp. vanilla extract
1/2 teasp. butter flavoring
1/2 teasp. almond extract
6 eggs whites
Cream Cheese Frosting*

Preheat oven to 350°. Grease and flour three (9-inch) round cake pans. In large mixing bowl, cream the butter and sugar until fluffy. Add flour, baking soda, baking powder, and salt. Pour in buttermilk and begin mixing slowly. Continue to mix until well blended. Add flavorings and stir. In a separate bowl, beat egg whites until stiff. Gently fold the egg whites into the cake batter. Divide the batter evenly between the three pans. Bake for 20 minutes at 350°, then lower heat to 300° and bake for about 25 minutes longer. Test doneness by inserting a toothpick near the center. Cake is done when toothpick comes out clean. Remove cakes from oven and cool on racks for ten minutes. After ten minutes, gently remove cakes from pans and continue cooling on racks to prepare for frosting. *See Cream Cheese Frosting recipe below.*

CREAM CHEESE FROSTING

8 ounce pkg. cream cheese
3 cups confectioners' sugar
2 teasp. vanilla extract

Combine ingredients in a mixing bowl and beat until smooth. Spread frosting between cooked layers and then on top and sides of cake. Serves 12 – 16.

CHESS PIE

1 cup sugar
3 eggs, beaten
1 stick butter

2 tabsp. flour
1 cup milk
1 teasp. vanilla

Cream butter and sugar; add flour, beaten eggs, milk and vanilla. Pour into unbaked pastry shell. Bake in 375° oven for about 30 minutes.

CHOCOLATE POUND CAKE

1 box yellow or butter recipe
cake mix
1 box chocolate instant
pudding mix
4 eggs
1/2 cup oil

1/2 cup ginger ale
1/2 cup chocolate mini morsels
1 (8 oz.) tub sour cream

Pre-heat oven to 350°. Mix cake and pudding mix, eggs, oil, ginger ale and chocolate morsels in medium bowl. On low speed, mix in sour cream. Spray Bundt cake pan with nonstick spray. Spoon in batter and bake at 350° for one hour. Cake is done when an inserted toothpick comes out clean.

BANANA PIE

Baked pie shell
3 bananas
1 cup milk
Whipped cream or Cool Whip

1 cup sour cream
1 pkg. instant vanilla pudding
mix

Slice three bananas into baked pie shell. Mix milk and sour cream; add vanilla pudding mix. Pour over bananas in shell. Cover with whipped cream or Cool Whip. Chill several hours. *Good and easy!*

Ya'll come for suppah, heah!

THE LADY IN RED

This is one of my favorite Mississippi stories. It actually happened on a Delta plantation, though parts of it remain a mystery. Here's the story as told by Bob Hardeman of Egypt Plantation near Greenwood…

Back in the spring of 1969, a work crew using a backhoe struck an object buried about three feet deep in the Delta soil. It was a mysterious, cast-iron box that had been partially cracked open by a backhoe, and out of the box ran a clear liquid. The workmen saw what was inside the box and they were incredulous. Someone ran to get Hardeman, and when he arrived, he was shocked to find a petite, perfectly preserved and well-dressed woman with long auburn hair and the clear, milky-white skin of a young woman. The style of her dress was unlike anything they'd ever seen. Her beautiful, well-made, red velvet dress was adorned with an exquisite white lace collar.

Hardeman immediately called the sheriff, who arrived about an hour later. In that short a time, the liquid preservative that covered her had leaked from the lead-lined coffin, and the lady in red had begun to change. Law enforcement officers and others conducted a major investigation to determine the identity of the "Lady in Red," to no avail. Some historians believe that her dress dates back to the mid-1800s, and the method of embalming also fits that time period.

It appears that the Lady in Red who died around 1835 had no one to claim her remains, for she has yet to be identified. According to Bob Hardeman, one plausible story is that she was on a boat on the nearby river that adjoins the and where she was found, and perhaps she died of yellow fever. There was a yellow fever pandemic about that time. Logically, they would put her off the boat out of fear of the deadly disease. She looked to be a woman of means because of her dress and because someone ordered her coffin from New Orleans then took great pains to preserve and bury her.

No record of her death has been found to this day, and so the mysterious "Lady in Red" has been formally laid to rest at the Odd Fellows Cemetery in nearby Lexington, Mississippi. Her marker reads: "Lady in Red. Found on Egypt Plantation. 1835 – 1969."

May she rest in peace.

Our Favorite Deep South Comfort Foods
and other recipes we love!

Food is a big part of life in the South. Whether it's Sunday dinner at grandmother's house, a family reunion or funeral, a picnic at the park, or tailgating at your favorite SEC football game, you'll find food in abundance. Sometimes, we just want to sit around a kitchen table and indulge in our favorite comfort foods. If we're having a bad day, we take comfort in forgetting about it while we focus on food. That's what you'll find below...foods in which we find comfort and can usually find at a gathering of friends and family. We hope you'll like them, too, and please don't think about diets, because some of these were popular before we became obsessed with weight and low-fat products.

MISSISSIPPI CAVIAR

2 (15 oz.) cans black-eye
  peas
2 small onions, thinly sliced
Black pepper, to taste
1 cup vegetable oil

1/4 cup wine vinegar
1 clove garlic, pressed
1/2 teasp. salt

Drain peas and layer with onions. Sprinkle each layer with pepper. Combine oil, vinegar, garlic and salt in blender; blend at high speed for three minutes, or until thoroughly blended. Pour over peas and onions; mix lightly. Refrigerate at least 24 hours. Will keep in refrigerator up to two weeks.

SUPERB CHEESE STRAWS

8 oz. extra sharp cheese
8 oz. sharp cheddar cheese
1-1/4 stick butter

2-1/2 cups all-purpose flour
1/8 teasp. cayenne pepper
1 teasp. salt

Grate cheese. Mix all ingredients well and put dough in cookie press. Use star point. Press on ungreased cookie sheet in two-inch strips. Bake at 300 degrees F. for about 15-20 minutes. Cheese straws freeze well.

BACON-ONION APPETIZERS

1/2 cup chopped green onion
  tops and roots
1 cup mayonnaise
12 slices bacon, well-dried
  and crumbled
Tabasco sauce to taste
  (or 1/2 teasp.)

1 teasp. paprika
Salt to taste (or about 1/4 teasp.)
Dash of pepper
Shredded wheat crackers

Mix all ingredients and spread on top of crackers. Broil until done, usually three to five minutes, but watch closely. Makes about 48 crackers.

HAM AND RED-EYE GRAVY

Place several slices of smoked ham in pre-heated black iron skillet. Brown ham on both sides, then reduce heat and fry slowly until ham sticks to the bottom. Remove ham from skillet and when skillet is very hot, add one cup of water. With a metal spatula or egg turner, scrape up the bits of ham stuck to the skillet. Stir, simmer for a few minutes, then serve with ham over grits, with eggs and biscuits. Great for brunch, or as a winter supper dish.

BROWNED BISCUIT

Cook biscuits or use the good frozen ones that come in a thick plastic bag. When cooked, cut biscuits in half. Heat syrup and butter in a skillet; place biscuits in skillet and brown on both sides. Serve with cup of hot coffee and a bowl of fruit for a delicious and quick Sunday supper dish.

ELEGANT AND EASY CRAB BISQUE

2 (7 oz.) cans crabmeat
2 cans tomato soup
1 can pea soup

2 cups heavy cream
2/3 cup dry sherry
Garnish: sour cream, chives

Flake crabmeat; heat with soups and cream, but do not boil. Stir in sherry; reheat. Garnish each serving with a tablespoon or so of sour cream. Sprinkle chives over all. Serves 8.

CATFISH IN PECANS

Catfish filets (4 to 6)
1 egg, beaten
Fajita seasoning
Flour (about 1/2 cup, on plate
  or flat surface

Lemon pepper seasoning
Ground pecans (about 1/2 cup)

Dip catfish filets in egg-milk mixture; roll fish in flour. Sprinkle with lemon pepper and fajita seasonings, then roll filet in ground pecans. Fry in vegetable oil quickly, but gently. Serves 4 – 6.

FAVORITE CHICKEN CASSEROLE

8 chicken breasts
2 cups dairy sour cream
2 (10-1/2) cans cream of
  chicken soup
1 cup chicken broth

2 tabsp. poppy seeds
1 (8 oz.) box Ritz crackers
3/4 cup butter

Boil chicken breasts until done; remove meat from bone. Mix next four ingredients. Crush crackers and mix with butter. Place layer of chicken, layer of crackers, layer of chicken and end with cracker layer. Bake one hour at 350° F. Serves 8.

COOKING TIP: Instead of a cooked turkey breast, use a 3-ounce serving of grilled chicken breast, grilled marinated tuna, canned water-packed tuna, grilled salmon, or grilled shrimp.

HEALTH TIP: Serve lots of steamed vegetables or delicious sliced tomatoes, peppers, or carrots. They provide nutrients with few calories and they dress up a plate of food. Vegetables are also rich in fiber and disease-fighting antioxidants.

MY MOTHER'S CORNBREAD DRESSING

- Boil fat hen, an onion and sliced celery stalk in salted water until tender; set aside, saving broth.
- Cook corn bread (To 1-1/2 cups self-rising corn meal, add one egg and about 1/2 to 3/4 cup of buttermilk; salt to taste. Bake in 400-degree oven until brown on top.)
- Crumble baked cornbread in large container, such as a roasting pan.
- Add four slices of white bread, coarsely torn.
- Add enough chicken broth to make mixture soft.
- Add one or two finely chopped onions to mixture.
- Add five hard-boiled eggs, chopped.
- Add three or four tablespoons of mayonnaise for added richness. If mixture is still dry, add more broth. Mixture must be soft or dressing will be dry.
- Add a pinch or two of sage, and salt and pepper to taste.
- Place fat hen on top of dressing and bake about one hour at 375° F.

Serves ten or twelve. *At Thanksgiving, my mother served sliced chicken and dressing with giblet gravy (see below), hot rolls, cranberry sauce, corn dish, green bean casserole, sweet potato casserole, broccoli and rice, congealed salad, green salad, deviled egg tray, and several desserts. Practically the same meal was served at Christmas, with the addition of a baked ham, asparagus, spiced apples, and red and green congealed salads.*

GIBLET GRAVY

To four tablespoons of chicken fat, add four tablespoons flour and brown slightly. While stirring, add two about cups chicken stock. Cook five minutes, add cut up giblets and one hard-boiled egg. Giblet gravy is served on top of dressing.

SOUTHERN FRIED CHICKEN

About 3/4 cup flour	1-1/2 teasp. paprika
Salt to taste	2 lb. fryer, cut-up
Pepper to taste	Crisco oil

Heat oil (or shortening if you prefer), which should be about a half inch deep in a black iron skillet. Place flour, salt, pepper and paprika in a brown paper bag; shake. Add a few pieces of chicken, then twist top of bag and shake to coat evenly. Do not crowd. If chicken is crowded, add more oil. Fry in hot oil until light brown on both sides. Reduce heat and cook 25 minutes longer. To "crisp" chicken, turn heat higher the last five minutes. Serve with gravy and creamed potatoes or rice.

CHICKEN GRAVY

This is essential to serve with Southern fried chicken! When chicken is done, remove from hot oil and allow to drain. Take about one or two tablespoons of fat from pan where chicken was fried (or pour off all but small amount from original skillet); place in a black iron skillet. Add one tablespoon of flour, salt and pepper, cook until brown. Mix equal amounts of milk and water, about one cup or more. Pour slowly into flour mixture. Stir and cook slowly until gravy is thick. Serve immediately over creamed potatoes or rice.

MARINATED VEGETABLE PLATTER

1/4 cup wine vinegar	1 hard-boiled egg, grated
1/4 cup salad oil	4 tabsp. chopped chives
1/2 cup mayonnaise	1 (16 oz.) can whole green beans
1-1/2 teasp. prepared mustard	1 (14-1/2 oz.) can asparagus
1/4 teasp. salt	spears
1/4 teasp. garlic powder	1 (14-1/2 oz.) can artichoke hearts
	1 (15 oz.) can Belgian carrots

Whisk together thoroughly the vinegar and oil. Add mayonnaise, mustard, salt and garlic powder and continue to whisk. Fold in egg and chives. Drain vegetables well and arrange separately in large glass baking dish; do not mix vegetables. Pour marinade over vegetables and refrigerate. To serve, arrange and decorate with sprigs of parsley. Serves about 16.

LYONNAISE CARROTS

2 small onions, minced	1/4 teasp. pepper
1/4 cup butter	4 cups cooked carrots
1/2 teasp. salt.	1 tabsp. minced parsley

Brown onion in butter; add salt, pepper and carrots. Cover and cook slowly about 20 minutes. Sprinkle with parsley. Serves 8.

ORANGE GLAZED SWEET POTATOES

6 medium sweet potatoes 2 tabsp. dark corn syrup
2 tabsp. butter 1 tabsp. grated orange peel
3/4 cup brown sugar 1/3 cup orange juice

Cut potatoes in quarters; cook until almost tender. Melt butter and brown sugar in skillet. Add syrup, orange peel and orange juice. Cook over low heat until mixture is slightly thickened. Stir occasionally. Add sweet potatoes and simmer about 30 minutes or until potatoes are glazed and tender. Serves 6.

ASPARAGUS CASSEROLE

2 (12 oz.) cans green 1/4 teasp. salt
  asparagus tips 1 tabsp. butter
1 small can tiny English peas Cheese sauce
1/2 cup slivered toasted almonds

Drain asparagus and English peas (save 1/2 cup liquid from asparagus for cheese sauce). Place in a greased baking dish in layers, with peas as the center layer. Sprinkle each layer with almonds and salt and dot with butter. Cover with cheese sauce.

CHEESE SAUCE: 3 tabsp. butter, 3 tabsp. flour, 1/4 teasp. salt, 1/8 teasp. butter, 1/2 cup milk, 1/2 cup asparagus liquid, I cup grated cheese. Melt butter over low heat; blend in flour until mixture is smooth. Cook until thickened, stirring constantly. Add 1/2 cup cheese and stir until melted. Pour over asparagus; top with remaining cheese. Bake at 375° F. for 20 – 25 minutes until brown. Serves 6 – 8.

GARLIC CHEESE GRITS

1 cup grits 1-1/2 tabsp. Worcestershire sauce
1 stick butter Tabasco sauce to taste
1 roll Kraft garlic cheese 2 egg whites

Cook grits according to package directions. Grits should not be runny. While hot, add butter, cheese, Worcestershire, and Tabasco. Allow to cool and fold in stiffly beaten egg whites. Pour into casserole and bake at 400 degrees F. for 20 minutes.

SKILLET CORNBREAD CASSEROLE

1 lb. lean ground beef	1/4 cup vegetable oil
2 eggs, beaten	2 cups Cheddar cheese
1 cup self-rising corn meal	1 lg. onion, chopped
1 can (16 oz.) cream style corn	2 to 4 jalapeño peppers, seeded and chopped
1 cup milk	

Crumble and brown ground beef; drain. Stir eggs, corn meal, cream style corn, milk and vegetable oil together. Pour one-half of the batter into greased black-iron skillet or 10-inch deep pie plate. Top evenly with browned ground beef followed by the grated cheese, onion and peppers. Pour remaining batter over the top. Bake in preheated 350° oven 45 to 55 minutes. Let stand five to 10 minutes before cutting into wedges to serve. Serves 6 to 8.

QUICK BANANA CAKE

1 pkg. white cake mix	1/2 cup water
2 eggs	1 cup mashed bananas

Combine all ingredients, beat thoroughly until smooth; turn into two cake pans that have been greased and floured. Bake at 350° for 25 – 30 minutes. Cool, frost with white or banana frosting.

EASY PARTY CAKE

Purchase one small angel food cake; slice crosswise in three even layers. Cook together until thick: one cup chopped dates, one cup water, 1/2 cup chopped walnuts. Cool. Spread this mixture between one layer, press down. Drain one can crushed pineapple and spread it between the other layer. Place in refrigerator several hours. About an hour before serving, cover cake with whipped cream. Serves 6.

BANANA PUDDIN'

2 doz. vanilla wafers
1/2 cup sugar
6 bananas
1 teasp. vanilla

1 pint milk
Pinch salt
3 eggs, separated

First, make a boiled custard of the milk, sugar and yolks of eggs. Add vanilla and salt. Place a layer of wafers then a layer of sliced bananas. Over this, put a portion of the custard. Repeat procedure until all is used, usually three layers, ending with bananas and custard on top. Make meringue of the three egg whites, using three extra tablespoons of sugar; put on top of pudding and bake in moderate over until brown, about ten minutes. Serve hot or cold.

PEACH ICE CREAM

8 eggs
4 cans condensed milk
2 cups sugar
3 quarts milk

2 tabsp. vanilla
2-1/2 cups fresh peaches, peeled,
  chopped
1 pint whipping cream

Combine first four ingredients. Mix thoroughly. Add condensed milk and regular milk. Mix, then add peaches. Refrigerate before freezing in ice cream freezer, overnight if possible, or long enough to cool ingredients. Then, freeze according to freezer instructions. Makes two gallons. *Note: Stawberries or bananas may be used instead of peaches. Very rich and very good!*

OLD FASHIONED LEMON ICE BOX PIE

1 vanilla wafer crust
1 can condensed milk
3 lemons for juice

1 grated lemon rind
3 eggs, separated

Make crust. Mix condensed milk and beat egg yolks. Add lemon juice. Pour in shell. Beat egg whites stiff. Add six tablespoons sugar. Pile on pie and brown 15 minutes. Cool and serve.

VANILLA WAFER CRUST: 1/2 cup vanilla wafers, finely crushed. 1/2 cup melted butter. Mix and press in pie plate. Chill.

CHOCOLATE POUND CAKE

1 box yellow cake mix
1 box chocolate instant
  pudding mix
4 eggs
1/2 cup chocolate mini morsels
1/2 cup oil

1/2 cup ginger ale
1 (8 oz.) container sour cream

Mix cake and pudding mix, eggs, oil, ginger ale and chocola/te morsels in medium bowl. On low speed, mix in sour cream as last ingredient. Spray Bundt cake pan with nonstick spray. Spoon in batter and bake in pre-heated 350-degree oven for one hour. Cake is done when an inserted toothpick comes out clean.

SUNSHINE CAKE
Delicious and so easy!

1 box yellow cake mix
3/4 cup water
4 eggs

1 box instant lemon pudding
3/4 cup oil

Mix all ingredients and bake in a 9 x 13 pan, as directed on box. When cake is done, while still hot, prick with fork and pour glaze (see below) over the top, covering it entirely.

GLAZE: 1/3 cup orange juice, 2 cups sifted powdered sugar, 2 teaspoons vanilla flavoring. Mix well.

GOOEY CAKE

1 stick butter, melted
1 egg
1 (8 oz.) pkg. cream cheese
1 box yellow cake mix
1 box confectioners sugar
2 eggs

Mix first three ingredients. Pat into greased pan. Mix next three ingredients and beat five minutes. Spread on cake mix in pan. Bake 30 minutes at 350°. *This recipe originated with Lillian Reynolds of Lillibet's Tea Room in Black Mountain, NC.*

LIFE'S LESSONS ...

TO HAVE A FRIEND,
BE A FRIEND, AND
ALWAYS KEEP A CONFIDENCE.

EVERY DAY ON EARTH IS A GIFT.
THAT'S WHY WE CALL EACH NEW DAY
"THE PRESENT."

IF A PROBLEM IS NOT LIFE-THREATENING,
IT'S NOT MAJOR.
IT'S JUST A SLIGHT GLITCH.

FROM CRISES COMES STRENGTH.

CONTACTS

ALABAMA

Special thanks to Ami Simpson of the Alabama Bureau of Tourism and Travel.

Alabama Bureau of Tourism
and Travel
Montgomery, AL
800-ALABAMA
Web: 800Alabama.com

Alexander City COC
256-234-3461
www.alexandercity.org

Auburn-Opelika CVB
866-880-8747
www.aocvb.com

Greater Birmingham CVB
800/458-8085
www.birminghamal.org

Cullman Area CVB
800/313-5114
www.cullmanchamber.org

Dauphin Island COC
877/532-8744
www.gulfinfo.com

Fairhope/Eastern Shore COC
251/928-6387
www.ESchamber.com

Florence/Lauderdale Tourism
888/FLO-TOUR
www.flo-tour.org

Gulf Shores
Alabama Gulf Coast CVB
251/968-6095
www.gulfshores.com

Huntsville/Madison County CVB
800-SPACE-4-U
www.huntsville.org

Mobile CVB
800-5-MOBILE
www.mobile.org

Montgomery Area Visitor Center
800/240-9452
www.visitingmontgomery.com

Selma & Dallas Co.
800-45-SELMA
www.SelmaAlabama.com

Talladega
256-362-9075
www.talladegachamber.com

Tuscaloosa CVB
800/538-8696
www.tcvb.org

Tuscumbia/Colbert Co. Tourism
800/344-0783
www.colbertcountytourism.org

Some attractions may require
specific directions, so we have
included their information in
event you wish to contact them
directly.

Dismals Canyon
Phil Campbell, AL
205/993-4559
www.dismalscanyon.com

Town of Mooresville
800/648-5381
www.northalabama.org

Mountain Top Flea Market
Attalla, AL
800/535-2286

Ave Maria Grotto
Cullman, AL
800/722-0999
www.avemariagrotto.com

Shrine of the Most Blessed
Sacrament of
Our Lady of the Angels
Monastery
Hanceville, Al (near Cullman)
256/352-6267
www.olamshrine.com

Robert Trent Jones Golf Trail
800/949-4444
www.visitrtjgolf.com

Chattahoochee Trace
Commission
Eufaula, AL
877-766-2443
www.hcc-al-ga.org

LOUISIANA

Special thanks to Jeff Richard of the Louisiana Office of Tourism.

Louisiana Office of Tourism
Baton Rouge, LA
800-99-GUMBO
Consumer Inquiries: 225/342-8119
www.LouisianaTravel.com

Abbeville Tourist Information Center
337/898-4264, 337/898-6600
www.vermilion.org

Alexandria/Pineville Area CVB
800/551-9546
www.louisianafromhere.com

Baton Rouge Area CVB
800/LA ROUGE, 225/382-3595
www.visitbatonrouge.com

Bayou Teche Visitors Center
Breaux Bridge
337/332-8500
www.breauxbridgelive.com

Bossier Visitor Center
Bossier City
318/45-VISIT

Cajun Coast Visitors &
Convention Bureau
Patterson
800/256-2931
www.cajuncoast.com

Houma Area CVB
800/688-2732

Iberia Parish CVB
New Iberia
888/942-3742
www.iberiatravel.com

Kenner CVB
800/231-5282
www.kennercvb.com

Lafayette CVB
800/346-1958
www.LafeyetteTravel.com

Lake Charles/Southwest
Louisiana CVB
800/456-7952
www.visitlakecharles.org

Morgan City Tourist Information Center
985/384-3343

Monroe/West Monroe CVB
800/843-1872
www.monroe-westmonroe.org

Natchitoches CVB
800/259-1714
www.natchitoches.net

New Orleans Metropolitan CVB
800/748-8695
www.neworleansinfo.com

New Orleans Tourism
888/239-3806
www.NewOrleansOnline.com

Opelousas Tourist Information
Center
800/424-5442
www.cityofopelousas.com

Ruston CVB
800/392-9032
www.RustonLincoln.com

Shreveport-Bossier Convention
& Tourist Bureau
888 45-VISIT, 318/222-9391
www.shreveport-bossier.org

St. Francisville Tourist Info.
888/307-8244
www.stfrancisville.us

St. Martinville Tourist Center
888/565-5939, 337/394-2233
www.st_matinville@hotmail.co

Louisiana Attractions Directory
225/346-1857
www.LouisianaAttractions.com

Louisiana State Parks and
Historic Sites
888/677-1400
www.LaStateParks.com

Louisiana Department of Wildlife
& Fisheries
225/765-2800
www.wlf.state.la.us

MISSISSIPPI

Special thanks to Steve Martin with the Mississippi Development Authority/Division of Tourism.

Mississippi Development
Authority/Tourism Division
Jackson, MS
866-SEE MISS (733-6477)
www.VisitMississippi.org

Bay St. Louis Tourism
Development
800/466-9048
www.hancockcountyms.org

Biloxi and Gulfport
MS Gulf Coast CVB
888/467-4853
www.gulfcoast.org

Canton CVB
800/844-3369
www.cantontourism.com

Clarksdale-Coahoma Co.
Tourism Commission
800/626-3764
www.clarksdaletourism.com

Cleveland COC/Tourism
800/295-7473
www.visitclevelandms.com

Columbus/Lowndes CVB
800/327-2686
www.columbus-ms.org

Corinth Tourism Promotion
Council
800/748-9048
www.corinth.net

Greenville CVB
800/467-3582
visitsgreenville.org

Greenwood CVB
800/748-9064
www.greenwoodms.org

Hattiesburg CVB
800/638-6877
www.hattiesburg.org

Holly Springs Tourism Bureau
662/252-2515
www.visithollysprings.org

Jackson CVB
800/354-7695
www.visitjackson.com

Laurel Tourism Council
877/GOLAUREL
www.laurelms.com

Meridian Tourism Bureau
888/868-7720
www.visitmeridian.com

Natchez CVB
800/647-6724
www.visitnatchez.com

Oxford Tourism Council
800/758-9177
www.touroxfordms.com

ABOUT THE AUTHOR

Sylvia Higginbotham is a native Mississippian, but she says she "hails from the South" because she's lived in the Southern states of Virginia, North Carolina, South Carolina, Florida, Louisiana and now Mississippi again. She worked in media and public relations the first fifteen years of her adult life and later managed three non-profits before she began writing full time.

Writing is not new to her, for she wrote her first travel article at the age of twelve. Since the mid 1980s, her articles have appeared in more than 150 newspapers and magazines and she has published nine non-fiction books. Additionally, Higginbotham has won numerous awards for work in television commercials and travel writing. She also writes documentaries and plays, and is waiting for the perfect time and age to finish a novel about Southern women.

She and her husband live in Columbus, Mississippi, but spend as much time as possible in the mountains of western North Carolina and elsewhere in the region in search of quaint and wonderful places down South. They are the parents of two adult daughters.